THE BIBLE

AND

MORMON SCRIPTURES COMPARED

PERMISSIONS

If not otherwise indicated, Scripture quotations are from the King James Bible.

Acknowledgement is made to the following who have granted permission for the reprinting of copyrighted material:

Quotations, as indicated, from New American Standard Bible, 1971, by permission of the Lockman Foundation, LaHabra, Calif., the copyright owner.

Permission is granted by Lincoln Christian Seminary, Lincoln, Ill., to reproduce Charles Crane's M.A. Thesis.

B. H. Roberts, ed., *History of the Church of Jesus Christ of the Latter-day Saints,* vols. 1-6; *Period I. History of Joseph Smith, The Prophet,* 4:461; *The Book of Mormon, Doctrine and Covenants, and Pearl of Great Price.* Permission granted by The Church of Jesus Christ of Latter-day Saints.

Religious Truths Defined, cited by Jerald Tanner and Sandra Tanner. Permission granted by Jerald Tanner and Sandra Tanner.

Photo reprints of *Doctrine and Covenants,* by permission of Jerald Tanner and Sandra Tanner, *Mormonism—Shadow or Reality?* Orson Pratt, *The Seer,* as cited with photo reprint by Jerald Tanner and Sandra Tanner, *Mormonism—Shadow or Reality?,* by permission of Jerald Tanner and Sandra Tanner.

John C. Trever, *The Untold Story of Qumran.* Permission by Fleming H. Revell Company.

"Apostle's Humor Draws Laughter," Permission granted by The Salt Lake Tribune.

T. B. Maston, *The Bible and Race* (Nashville: Broadman Press, 1959). Used by permission.

Joseph Fielding Smith, *Doctrines of Salvation.* Permission granted by Bookcraft, Salt Lake City, Utah.

THE BIBLE

AND

MORMON SCRIPTURES COMPARED

or

The Educational Process of Winning Mormons

by

Dr. Charles Arthur Crane

College Press, Joplin, Missouri

Second Printing 1977
Third Printing 1979
Revised Edition 1983
Fifth Printing 1989
Sixth Printing 1992

Printed and Bound in the
United States of America

Library of Congress Catalog Card Number: 83-72713
International Standard Book Number: 0-89900-196-3

ACKNOWLEDGEMENTS

It would seem ungrateful to not mention the people who have been a great help in such a work as this. Probably no other persons have compiled so much resource material as Jerald and Sandra Tanner, who have printed over twenty volumes dealing with the history and practices of the Mormon Church. Their friendship over the past nine years has been a great encouragement. They have graciously given permission to quote from their materials as desired.

Another person who has been a great help is Marvin Cowan. Marvin has lectured all over America on the subject of the Mormon system. He has many deep insights into the problems and doctrine of the Latter-day Saints. Our mutual encounters with the leaders of the Mormon Church were not only interesting but informative.

Many of the materials shared in this manuscript have come from actual encounters with the Mormon people. The Mormon people, themselves, have served as a proving ground for this approach to teaching and winning Mormon people to Christ.

My wife, Margaret, has always been ready to help me, not only in typing the manuscript and checking the style, but patiently sitting at home many evenings while I talked with the Mormon people. It would be impossible to give her the credit that is due her.

And finally I would like to remember my good friends, Dr. Robert Wilson and President Charles Mills of Lincoln Christian Seminary, who helped in reading and adjusting the manuscript.

ABOUT THE AUTHOR

Dr. Charles A. Crane was raised in the State of Oregon and has been heavily involved in the work of the church most of his life. He began preaching at the age of nineteen and continues as a preaching minister at this time.

He has a fine theological education that qualifies him to write such a book. He has the earned degrees of: Bachelor of Sacred Literature, Master of Arts, Master of Divinity and Doctor of Ministry as well as a degree in psychology.

He has spent over thirty years researching Mormon history and doctrine. His first encounter with Mormonism came at the age of 13 when he became friends with a Mormon neighbor and later worked for him. His next job, at age 16, was for another Mormon man. This man had advanced positions with the L.D.S. church and they had a number of discussions about Mormon doctrine. This further prompted his interest and study of the subject. During college days he was again cast in with Mormon people. He became friends with Larry Jonas and together they encountered the missionaries and continued their studies.

His first ministry at Sutherlin, Oregon, again threw him among L.D.S. people. When the opportunity came to minister with a small New Testament church in Salt Lake City, it seemed as if God had been preparing him for this work. This church grew to be one of the most prosperous non-Mormon churches in Utah during the seven years of his ministry there. Two other New Testament churches were begun in Utah. There were many L.D.S. people won to Christ during this time.

The author has led several hundred L.D.S. people to Christ and continues to write, teach and lecture on this subject around the country. Included in this large number of converts have been several who held the highpriesthood. One of these had been on two adult missions and had served as a Temple guide.

During the years when few people were warning of the errors of Mormon doctrine, he has stood and clearly shown its errors.

Many today have joined in this important work. He continues today, motivated by his strong love for Mormon people, warning those shackled by these false doctrines.

His prayer is that this material, which has blessed so many, might be a help to you.

TABLE OF CONTENTS

INTRODUCTION

Some might wonder why one would say anything against another religion. Why pick on someone's religion or church? What sort of spirit would make one want to tear down another's doctrine or church? In explanation I would reply: there is only one church, the Church of the Lord Jesus Christ. This church is made up of all true obedient believers in Christ. It has always included all of the saved, from the beginning of the church until the present day. This church has, as Christ predicted, been beset with false teachers. It is the responsibility of its leaders to plead for correct doctrine. Those who accept this responsibility are not seeking to tear down the church, but to preserve and strengthen it. If men have started churches that teach doctrines contrary to the things taught by Christ and His Apostles, then yes, we should seek to destroy all of these false teachings and organizations. Any true Christian would.

My interest in the study of the Latter-day Saints (L.D.S. or Mormons) began when I was fourteen years old. I had been building fence for my father on our farm when a neighbor who saw the straight fences that I had built asked me to work for him. I accepted the job and received five dollars a day for eight hours of fence building or other hard farm work. I came to love this fine man, Homer Moxley, during the time I was employed by him. We became fast friends. He was a Latter-day Saint and we had several long discussions about his beliefs. In the process of time Homer left the Mormon Church and professed his faith in Jesus Christ alone.

At the age of sixteen I acquired a job working at O & M Tire Shop near my home town. The owner of this business was Lowell C. Funk. Lowell and I became good friends and remain so to this day. Lowell was an official in the organization of the Latter-day Saint Church in that district in Oregon. Lowell was a very staunch Mormon. We had many friendly discussions about his faith and church. Lowell later attended some of my public lectures on Mormonism. I personally believe that Lowell's faith in the Mormon system was shaken, but due to family ties, an influential position, and other reasons he has never left the Mormon Church. These discussions with him helped to broaden my comprehension of Mormon doctrine and practice.

While in college I worked part time for Goodyear Tire and Rubber Company. I became friends with Dean Adams, a fellow employee of Goodyear. Dean was a strong Mormon and sought to win me to the Mormon faith. During this time I was reading and studying the Mormon system, comparing it with scripture. Dean was never won to the Lord, but he did learn to respect our position and asked not to discuss the subject further with me.

After graduation from college and ordination to the ministry, I was called to my first church in Sutherlin, Oregon. There was an active Latter-day Saint Church there, and it was only a short time before we were having some serious discussions with their people. One of the young men was a missionary who had parents and other relatives living there. During these talks we baptized the missionary's parents, aunt and uncle, and sister and brother-in-law. Further contact with their leaders was limited as they evaded us. Whenever we had contact with them they retreated. For several years though, we remained friends with the young missionary.

When, in January of 1966, the opportunity came to minister to the very small Southeast Christian Church in Salt Lake City, Utah, we felt that God had prepared us and was leading us to a ministry in that great city. During the seven years of our ministry we had numerous contacts with the Mormons. We talked with the missionaries, bishops, ward teachers, and with any other person when we had the opportunity. I was never able to talk personally with a prophet of the Mormon Church but during this time did have occasion to converse with two of their apostles.

Our ministry in Utah was very fruitful. The church membership grew from ninety to well over six hundred. The Southeast Church started two other New Testament churches in the Salt Lake Valley. One other independent church joined with the movement to restore the New Testament church. There were over two hundred Mormons who left their faith and were baptized into Christ. The Southeast Church was, and continues to be, one of the most prosperous non-Mormon churches in the state of Utah. It recently received an award as the fastest growing church in Utah.

When we first moved to Utah, the Latter-day Saint people would hardly give me time to study for my sermons. They made every effort to win me to their faith. The missionaries came to my house and office. I was invited to lunch by business people, where

I would again hear their story.

I recognized the need for further study and began to read extensively about the Mormon Church and its history. I studied The Book of Mormon and Doctrine and Covenants. During this period my reading included books both for and against the system. It wasn't long before the bishops and missionaries began to evade me. Whenever I called on a new person in the neighborhood the Mormons would quit calling on them. I couldn't get a session with them. (This was after we had had several sessions with the local bishops and seminary instructors.) During this time there were five families on our street won to Christ.

Opportunities to lecture on the subject have come from several states, conventions, and colleges.

From the beginning I have loved the people. They have so many fine traits. I still have many good Mormon friends today. We have always maintained a good relationship with them. I respect them and they me. There are many good things that can be said about these hard working, clean, honest people. Of course, as in other churches, some of them are not good people, but for the most part I have found them fine people.

This does not mean that they have the truth. In fact, I have found no religious body in America further from the truth. A Muslim is more nearly a Christian than a knowledgeable Mormon who believes all their doctrines about God and Christ.

Thousands of requests have come for a summary of the things that have been found to be most helpful in winning these people. It is with much prayer and a deep concern that I send forth these words.

A WORD OF CAUTION

The Apostle warns, "Knowledge makes arrogant, but love edifies," I Corinthians 8:1. There is a real and serious danger that we only prepare so we can "put down" L.D.S. people. Such an attitude will not be fruitful for our Lord.

It is only love that gives us the right to share with any Mormon person our faith. They will not listen to any other approach and should not. The truth, shared in love, may produce in them an initial response of frustration and anger. Yet, when we have the Spirit of Christ we will persist in being kind and loving.

It is necessary to show the L.D.S. person the error of the Mormon system. This will take a lot of careful, prayerful research on your part. But remember information without love is dead.

Several things must be in your own life before you are ready to share with a Mormon friend.

1. Godliness. A complete surrender of your life to Christ.

2. Prayer. Trusting that God will work through you.

3. Friendship. This must be genuine. It may take years to earn the right to be heard.

4. Patience. To share too much too soon can be offensive. Help them to think. When that has happened they are on their way to Christ. Few L.D.S. persons have ever come to Christ quickly.

5. Truth. We are in search of truth.

Therefore the material in this paper is to be used with caution. When you are ready to share in love begin by opening a conversation with a Mormon friend. Share patiently. Many of the L.D.S. people whom the author led to Christ took as much as five years.

We need to remember that L.D.S. people are not the enemy, but are victims of the enemy. What they need to hear first is the music of the gospel lived out in our lives. Then they will be ready to listen to the words of the gospel.

May God bless you in your efforts to share our Lord. Prayerfully, I submit these thoughts on why the Book of Mormon is not scripture, but a fairy tale.

Dr. Charles A. Crane, 1983

Part I

THE BIBLE AND MORMON SCRIPTURES COMPARED

Chapter I

"FOR EVER, O LORD, THY WORD IS SETTLED IN HEAVEN." *Psalms 119:89*

It is so important for us to know what is and what is not scripture. Are we to accept Joseph Smith and the later prophets of the Latter-day Saints in their claims of being inspired of God? Are they inspired? Can we tell? Do the Scriptures of the Latter-day Saints really stand as equal with the Bible? These are questions that every Latter-day Saint should carefully consider. If, in truth, the extra Mormon scriptures measure up to the standard of the Bible, then we need to know this so we can profit from them.

In the beginning, we should examine the evidence in support of the accuracy of the Bible. The Bible's history is long and interesting. In recent years much has happened to enlighten us as to the history of the Bible. There have been many fascinating new manuscript discoveries. We wish to examine several of these manuscripts.

The Bible, being such an ancient book, has an interesting history. The books of Moses, Genesis through Deuteronomy, date back nearly fifteen hundred years before the time of Christ. The last of the prophetical books of the Old Testament was written at least four hundred years before Christ. Our New Testament Scriptures date from approximately A.D. 50 to A.D. 98. So we are dealing with an ancient book when we deal with the Bible. Since the Bible has aroused not only much love, but also much hatred its history has been thoroughly studied with a view to either prove or disprove it. We hope to examine a little of this area of study.

One of the accusations that is often made by the Mormon critic of the Bible is that it has had many plain and precious parts removed. In fact, Joseph Smith, Jr. made such a statement. "I believe the Bible as it read when it came from the pen of the original writers. Ignorant translators, careless transcribers, or designing and corrupt priests have committed many errors."[1]

Other Mormon leaders have made similar accusations against the Bible's accuracy. A son of Joseph Fielding Smith, recent Prophet of the Latter-day Saints Church, made the following statement about the Bible.

> Scholars do not deny that the original text of the Bible has been corrupted. Truths have been removed to preserve traditions. Faulty translations and omissions of phrases and clauses have resulted in confusion.[2]
>
> The early "Apostate Fathers" did not think it was wrong to tamper with the inspired scripture. If any scripture seemed to endanger their viewpoint, it was altered, transplanted, or completely removed from the Biblical text. All this was done that they might keep their traditions. Such mutilation was considered justifiable to preserve the "purity" of their doctrines.[3]

Even The Book of Mormon claims that the Bible has been tampered with and changed.

> ...for behold, they have taken away from the gospel of the Lamb many parts which are plain and most precious; and also many covenants of the Lord have they taken away. And all this have they done that they might pervert the right ways of the Lord, that they might blind the eyes and harden the hearts of the children of men.[4]

Now the point under consideration is, Are these statements true? Can we check and know? The evidence must be considered. We would like to examine the facts so that we can know beyond any shadow of doubt the answer to these questions. The evidence is plentiful.

Let's begin with the Old Testament. The best proof that can be brought forth is of fairly recent origin, the Dead Sea Scrolls. The Dead Sea Scrolls were found in four caves near the northwest end of the Dead Sea at a place called Qumran. Many of these documents now rest in the museum in Jerusalem called the Dome of the Scroll of the Book. This building is located near the Kenesset building. Its roof is shaped like a scroll jar lid. Inside this small, climate-controlled building are displayed for viewing the Dead

---

[1] B. H. Roberts, ed., *History of The Church of Jesus Christ of Latter-day Saints*, vols. 1-6: *Period I. History of Joseph Smith, The Prophet*, by Joseph Smith; vol. 7: *Period II. From the Manuscript History of Brigham Young and Other Original Documents;* 7 vols., 2nd ed. (Salt Lake City, Utah: Deseret News Press, 1963), 6:57

[2] *Religious Truths Defined*, p. 337, cited by Jerald Tanner and Sandra Tanner, *Mormonism—Shadow or Reality?* (Salt Lake City, Utah: Modern Microfilm Co., 1964), p. 64.

[3] *Religious Truths Defined*, p. 175, cited by Jerald Tanner and Sandra Tanner, *Mormonism—Shadow or Reality?*, p. 64.

[4] The Book of Mormon, I Nephi 13:26b-27.

Sea manuscripts. Every Old Testament book is found among the Dead Sea Scrolls with the exception of the book of Esther.

Conservative scholars have dated these manuscripts from 325 B.C. to 100 B.C. Most Biblical manuscripts have been dated about 225 B.C. These manuscripts were found from 1946 to 1960. The first manuscript was found when a shepherd boy threw a rock into a cave and heard a jar break. His curiosity led to the discovery of the first scrolls. The events of the finding and examination of the documents are very interesting but are not important to our study.

The important question is, Have these documents proved our Old Testament scriptures to be changed? The answer is an emphatic, no! The oldest manuscript that we had before this time, of any Hebrew Old Testament book, had been dated A.D. 916. It was the Leningrad Codex and is in the Leningrad Royal Library in Russia. One other partial manuscript of the first five books of the Bible may date around A.D. 840. These are Hebrew manuscripts. Therefore, when the Dead Sea Scrolls were found they were supremely important in establishing the accuracy of our Old Testament text.

When the American scholar, Dr. John C. Trever, first found and read the Isaiah Scroll and compared it with the oldest Hebrew manuscripts, he was disappointed in that they were the same. He said they shed no new light. They only established that the Hebrew text had come down over one thousand years with remarkable accuracy. For all practical reasons the later one was as accurate as the earlier, establishing the fidelity of our Hebrew text. Dr. Trever says, "Thus, as has been repeatedly stated, the ancient Isaiah Scroll is a witness to the antiquity and faithful preservation of the traditional Masoretic text from at least as early as the first century B.C."[5] Dr. Trever later explains in his book how the Daniel Scroll confirmed the accuracy of the manuscripts we already had.

> With the sixth layer removed, the remainder of the largest fragment was revealed. Now parts of Daniel 3:22-31 (3:22—4:1 in English) had appeared on two fragments. Having impressed me at first as revealing a script somewhat similar to the Manual of Discipline (IQS), I tentatively thought of the

---

5 John C. Trever, *The Untold Story of Qumran* (Westwood, New Jersey: Fleming H. Revell Company, 1952), p. 117.

> fragments as belonging to the middle of the first century B.C. Although the text contributed nothing new, its significance among Biblical manuscripts was immediately apparent.[6]

I have personally seen these Hebrew documents. They are remarkably clear and readable. They give us positive proof that the Old Testament scriptures have come down to us remarkably preserved. Many of the statements from past times, such as the one we quoted by Joseph Smith, are outdated and inaccurate in the light of recent manuscript discoveries. A knowledgeable scholar of the Bible today would not ever make the statement that many plain and precious truths have been removed from the Old Testament scriptures.

When we realize the carefulness of the Old Testament scribes in transcribing their scriptures, we are not surprised that the Bible is extremely accurate. The Talmud gave the following rules to govern the preparation of a Manuscript to be used in the synagogue.

> 1. The parchment must be made from the skin of clean animals; must be prepared by a Jew only, and the skins must be fastened together by strings taken from clean animals. 2. Each column must have no less than 48 nor more than 60 lines. The entire copy must be first lined, and if three words were written in it without the line, the copy was worthless. 3. The ink must be of no other color than black, and it must be prepared according to a special recipe. 4. No word nor letter could be written from memory; the scribe must have an authentic copy before him, and he must read and pronounce aloud each word before writing it. 5. He must reverently wipe his pen each time before writing the word for "God," and he must wash his whole body before writing the word "Jehovah," lest the holy name be contaminated. 6. Strict rules were given concerning the forms of the letters, spaces between letters, words, and sections, the use of the pen, the color of the parchment, etc. 7. The revision of a roll must be made within 30 days after the work was finished; otherwise it was worthless. One mistake on a sheet condemned the sheet; if three mistakes were found on any page, the entire manuscript was condemned. 8. Every word and every letter was counted, and if a letter were omitted, an extra letter inserted, or if one letter touched another, the manuscript was condemned and destroyed at once. And so on. Some of these rules may appear extreme and absurd, yet they show how sacred the Holy Word of the Old Testament was to its custodians, the Jews (Romans 3:2), and they give us strong encouragement to believe that we have the real Old Testament, the same one which our Lord had and which was originally given by inspiration by God.[7]

---

[6] *Ibid.*, p. 129.

[7] H. S. Miller, *General Biblical Introduction* (Houghton, New York: The Word-Bearer Press, 1959), pp. 184-185.

One would expect to find that there were very few places where there were mistakes or differences of real significance. The Dead Sea Scrolls have given us undeniable proof of the accuracy of our Old Testament scriptures. The evidence is so remarkable that it appears that God has taken special pains to show us, in the last days, that His word, the Bible, is accurate. Christians ought to be grateful for this added testimony to the fidelity of the Old Testament Scriptures.

An examination of the New Testament discloses even more remarkable evidence to support its accuracy. In fact, there are over 3,500 Greek manuscripts of New Testament books.

The oldest New Testament manuscript is a partial, fragmentary copy called the Chester Beatty Papyri.

> The Chester Beatty Papyri is the greatest discovery of the new Biblical manuscripts, at least since the Freer collection, and possibly since the Codex Sinaiticus, was made.... All the manuscripts are on papyrus, in codex form, and of an early date, from the 2nd to the 5th century; in fact, the really Biblical manuscripts are, with one exception, dated in the 2nd and 3rd century [8].

It is possible that portions of this manuscript may date back into the year 150 or earlier. If this is true, then it is of great value. If its date was A.D. 250, still it is wonderful proof of what the Bible was like at that time. This manuscript fragment contains nine epistles, almost complete, and in the following order: Romans, Hebrews, First and Second Corinthians, Ephesians, Galatians, Philippians, Colossians, and First Thessalonians.

This manuscript also gives us proof that at a very early date these documents were bound together in a common book. They also prove that our later editions of the Bible were extremely accurate.

A second proof that the New Testament scriptures have not been changed and revised is the Bodmer II Text of the Gospel of John. This manuscript is kept in the Vatican Library in Rome. It is dated, by able scholars, in the year A.D. 200. Since the Gospel of John was written about A.D. 95 this document takes us back within 105 years of the time that John wrote it.

It is remarkable that we find no substantial change in the later

---

[8] *Ibid.*, p. 200.

copies. It proves that the Gospel of John has not been tampered with, changed, or revised.

There are four major, complete, Greek manuscripts of the Bible that give us firm proof of its accuracy. These are the Sinaitic (Codex Sinaiticus) which was written in A.D. 340; the Vatican (Codex Vaticanus) which is dated in the year A.D. 325; the Alexandrian (Codex Alexandrinus) dated about A.D. 450; and the Ephraem (Codex Ephraemi Rescriptus) which is also dated about A.D. 450.

These four documents are Greek, clear and readable, and in substantial agreement as to the New Testament text. They also contain the Old Testament in Greek.

It is true that in later manuscript copies we have textual problems. It has been estimated that there may be as many as 300,000 textual problems or variations. At first glance this seems astounding, but after a moment's thought it is amazing that there aren't more. Since there are between three and four thousand manuscripts, if there were only one difference between each of them there would immediately be three to four thousand textual problems. Thus, there are really less than one hundred problem passages. In fact, the really significant textual problems narrow down to less than twenty. Substantial agreement is found between the older copies, while variations appear in the later. Careful examination shows that the twenty or less textual problems do not involve any important doctrinal issues. While one passage might be questioned, another nonquestioned passage says a similar thing.

Many of the textual problems center around marginal notes, fragmentary ends of books, unclear copy work, and the like. It is astounding that out of so many copies in Greek we would produce so few real textual problems and then find that nothing doctrinal can be brought into question by the problems. Modern scholarship has established our New Testament scriptures beyond question.

Joseph Smith did not have sufficient education to make such a charge as he does about the Bible. The fact that he does accuse the Bible of gross inaccuracies, while scholarship has shown his accusation to be false, places him in a very uncertain place as a supposed prophet of God.

Chapter II

"HEAVEN AND EARTH SHALL PASS AWAY: BUT MY WORDS SHALL NOT PASS AWAY."

Mark 13:31

Most Bible writers claim for themselves inspiration. We find this true from Moses throughout the rest of the Bible. There is a certainty about their message that gives it a ring of authenticity. For example, God said to Moses, "And the Lord said unto Moses, Write this for a memorial in a book, and rehearse it in the ears of Joshua: for I will utterly put out the remembrance of Amalek from under heaven."[1] When the Ten Commandments were given it was said: "And the Lord said unto Moses, Come up to me into the mount, and be there: and I will give thee tables of stone, and a law, and commandments which I have written; that thou mayest teach them."[2] There is a certainty about the writings of Moses; we can have little doubt that he spoke from God. We could give other instances in his writings. For example, examine Exodus 34:27, Numbers 17:2-3, and Deuteronomy 31:9.

This type of statement is repeatedly made throughout the entire Old Testament scriptures. Whether it be Joshua, David, Solomon, Isaiah, Jeremiah, or any of the rest of the prophets, each emphatically claims inspiration for himself. We never find words of doubt about what they write. They write with a certainty seldom found in literature.

These men, very evidently, wrote under a promise similar to that made to Moses. When Moses sought to be excused from the work he was to do, God said to him that He would guide and direct him.

> And Moses said unto the Lord, O my Lord, I am not eloquent, neither heretofore, nor since thou hast spoken unto thy servant: but I am slow of speech, and of a slow tongue. And the Lord said unto him, Who hath made man's mouth? or who maketh the dumb, or deaf, or the seeing, or the blind? have not I the Lord? Now therefore go, and I will be with thy mouth, and teach thee what thou shalt say.[3]

---

[1] Exodus 17:14.

[2] Exodus 24:12.

[3] Exodus 4:10-12.

Thus, each of the writers was positive about his message and his source of material. This is not so in the Book of Mormon. There is much uncertainty. This will be covered further in chapter three.

The New Testament scriptures further undergird this teaching of inspiration of God. Not only the Apostles but Jesus himself affirms the inspiration of the Old Testament.

To quote Jesus: "And he said unto them, These are the words which I spake unto you, while I was yet with you, that all things must be fulfilled which were written in the law of Moses, and in the prophets, and in the psalms, concerning me."[4] This is a firm statement of the inspiration of the Old Testament writers, as they could have only known about Jesus through the avenue of inspiration. On another occasion Jesus said, "the scriptures cannot be broken."[5] To insist that the scriptures can indeed be broken, or are fallible, is to reject the divinity of Jesus.

The Apostles are equally clear as to the infallibility of the scriptures, both Old and New Testaments. We might begin with a passage from the book of Hebrews. This passage is quoted from the New American Standard Version because the terminology of the King James is hard to understand. "God, after He spoke long ago to the fathers in the prophets in many portions and in many ways, in these last days has spoken to us in His Son, whom He appointed heir of all things, through whom also He made the worlds."[6] This is an endorsement of the Old and New Testaments at once. God spoke through the prophets. God spoke through His Son. It would be hard to miss the meaning of this clear passage which asserts the inspiration of the Old and New Testaments.

Paul, writing to Timothy, makes it abundantly clear about the matter of the inspiration of the scriptures. "All scripture is given by inspiration of God, and is profitable for doctrine, for reproof, for correction, for instruction in righteousness: That the man of God may be perfect, thoroughly furnished unto all good works."[7]

---

4 Luke 24:44

5 John 10:35.

6 Hebrews 1:1-2, New American Standard Version.

7 II Timothy 3:16-17.

Peter leaves no doubt about the matter of the inspiration of the scriptures when he says:

> Of which salvation the prophets have enquired and searched diligently, who prophesied of the grace that should come unto you: Searching what, or what manner of time the Spirit of Christ which was in them did signify, when it testified beforehand the sufferings of Christ, and the glory that should follow. Unto whom it was revealed,...[8]

Such clear statements about inspiration are a great help in a study such as this.

Are we to suppose that the God that made the universe, who created mankind, made man able to communicate with one another, is incapable of communicating with mankind in an accurate, intelligent way? So the Old and New Testament writers repeatedly claim that God had used this means to communicate with mankind.

A God of such power as to make the universe, keep it running, and order this creation in such an intelligent manner, is capable of giving a revelation that is consistent, not needing changes, and free of errors. Certainly for man to write such a book would be impossible. But we would expect just such a book from God. Anything less would be a disappointment.

Several other passages inform us about the inspiration of the Bible. One Old Testament passage should be included in such a summary of scripture.

> Now these be the last words of David. David the son of Jesse said, and the man who was raised up on high, the anointed of the God of Jacob, and the sweet psalmist of Israel, said, The Spirit of the Lord spake by me, and his word was in my tongue.[9]

God used men, giving them the power to receive and communicate divine truth. God used their own personalities, but guarded them from error, enabling them to speak His words in their own style.

Peter sums up the matter well when he says,

> We have also a more sure word of prophecy; whereunto ye do well that ye take heed, as unto a light that shineth in a dark place, until the day dawn, and the day star arise in your hearts: Knowing this first, that no prophecy of the scripture is of any private interpretation. For the prophecy came not in old time by the will of man: but holy men of God spake as they were moved by the Holy Ghost.[10]

---

[8] I Peter 1:10-12.

[9] II Samuel 23:2.

[10] II Peter 1:19-20.

Thus, we can safely say that the Bible writers spoke by the power of God. This explains why the Bible is accurate, when it speaks about medicine, when it speaks about science, when it speaks about history, human nature, spiritual truth, or any other subject.

This explains why Bible writers could predict such events as the coming of Christ with such remarkable accuracy. This explains how David would be able to write the twenty-second Psalm that tells about Jesus' crucifixion. This tells us why Daniel knew about the four great world empires that he writes about in the second chapter of Daniel. This explains how Daniel knew that Jesus would come at the time He predicted He would in Daniel 9:24-27. We understand how Isaiah could write the fifty-third chapter of Isaiah which tells so much about Jesus. When we begin to comprehend inspiration, we know how John could write Revelation, that great book of history, written in advance of history. All of this is because "holy men of God spake as they were moved by the Holy Ghost."[11]

Sometimes these men didn't even understand what they had written. Many examples of this could be given such as Peter's sermon in Acts, where he says this salvation was to "all that are afar off."[12] Then later, in the tenth chapter of Acts, God had to work a miracle or two to get Peter to accept what he had already preached.

The Old Testament prophets desired to know more about what they spoke but were not allowed to do so. They were curious, but God only gave them a partial view of what was to come.

> Of which salvation the prophets have inquired and searched diligently, who prophesied of the grace that should come unto you: Searching what, or what manner of time the Spirit of Christ which was in them did signify, when it testified beforehand the sufferings of Christ, and the glory that should follow. Unto whom it was revealed, that not unto themselves, but unto us they did minister the things, which are now reported unto you by them that have preached the gospel unto you with the Holy Ghost sent down from heaven; which things the angels desire to look into.[13]

So not only did Jesus claim inspiration for the Bible writers

---

[11] II Peter 1:21.

[12] Acts 2:39.

[13] I Peter 1:10-12.

and they themselves claim that they were inspired, the works that they produced prove beyond any doubt that they were in truth inspired of God.

Chapter III

A TEXT CRITICAL COMPARISON OF THE BIBLE AND BOOK OF MORMON

"*...try the spirits whether they are from God: because many false prophets are gone out into the world.*" I John 4:1

The big question is, does the Book of Mormon measure up to the standards of the Bible? What does a critical examination of the texts of both show? Is the Book of Mormon scientifically, historically, and factually sound? These questions need to be answered.

A brief explanation of the Book of Mormon seems wise for those who are not familiar with it. The Book of Mormon claims to be a book much like the Bible. In fact, it has recently been called The Second New Testament. It covers a period of time from 600 B.C. to A.D. 421. It is a series of books telling of the life and descendants of Lehi, a man of Jerusalem. It is a series of claimed revelations and historical accounts given by men during this thousand year period of time.

Joseph Smith, Jr. said that he was told about the book by God, who directed him to find it and translate it from the golden plates upon which it had been written. The work of translation was accomplished by Joseph Smith wearing some divine glasses and looking into these in a hat. As he translated the material and had it recorded by his scribe, to God's satisfaction, the image in the glasses would fade away and a new image would come in its place. The three witnesses bear testimony to the accuracy of the fact of the gold plates and that they were translated into English by Joseph Smith, Jr.

> Be It Known unto all nations, kindreds, tongues, and people, unto whom this work shall come: That we, through the grace of God the Father, and our Lord Jesus Christ, have seen the plates which contain this record, which is a record of the people of Nephi, and also of the Lamanites, their brethren, and also of the people of Jared, who came from the tower of which hath been

spoken. And we also know that they have been translated by the gift and power of God, for his voice hath declared it unto us; wherefore we know of a surety that the work is true.[1]

The claims for the Bible and the Book of Mormon are quite different. The Bible claims to be inspired, as written by its original writers. Since that time it has been copied and recopied and translated numerous times. The remarkable thing about the Bible is that, though it has come from ancient times, its accuracy has been remarkably preserved.

As we carefully observe both books we want to do so as fairly as possible. We want to ask ourselves constantly this question, is this an actual record of actual fact? The plan will be to lay each book along side each other and along side of the evidence. In each event, we will look first at the Bible and then at the Book of Mormon.

THE BIBLE AND BOOK OF MORMON STATEMENTS ABOUT THEMSELVES

The Bible's Statement About Itself

"Forever, O Lord, Thy word is settled in heaven," Psalms 119:89, and "The sum of Thy word is truth, And every one of Thy righteous ordinances is everlasting," Psalms 119:160, N.A.S.V. In any mathematical equation an error in any part of the calculation causes an inaccurate sum or total. This passage of Scripture affirms that if one sums up all of the teachings of the Word of God it will total "truth." It is like Jesus said in John 10:35 "...the Scripture cannot be broken,...." Paul said,

All Scripture is inspired by God and profitable for teaching, for reproof, for correction, for training in righteousness; that the man of God may be adequate, equipped for every good work. II Timothy 3:16-17 N.A.S.V.

The Book of Mormon's Statements About Itself

Nevertheless, I do not write anything upon plates save it be that I think[2] it be sacred. And now, if I do err, even did they err of old; not that I would excuse myself because of other men, but because of the weakness which is in me, according to the flesh, I would excuse myself. I Nephi 19:6

---

[1] *The Book of Mormon, The Testimony of Three Witnesses*, p. vii.

[2] Underlining supplied by author for emphasis throughout the book.

or again,

> And I, Lehi, according to the things which I have read, must needs suppose that an angel of God, according to that which is written, had fallen from heaven; wherefore, he became a devil, having sought that which was evil before God. II Nephi 2:17

There is an interesting comparison between the sureness of the Bible as compared to the uncertainty of the Book of Mormon. Many more illustrations could be given to show the certainty of the Bible and the uncertainty of the Book of Mormon.

TEXTUAL MANUSCRIPT EVIDENCE FOR THE BIBLE AND BOOK OF MORMON

Textual Evidence for the Bible[3]

Textual Evidence for the Book of Mormon

What is the textual manuscript evidence for the Book of Mormon? The Mormon Church has the original handwritten copy of the Book of Mormon as made by the scribes as reportedly dictated by Joseph Smith. This handwritten copy is in the archives of the church and not available for us to study. All that is available to the critic is a photo reprint of the original printed edition of the Book of Mormon, 1830 edition. This is called, "Joseph Smith Begins His Works, Volume 1," printed by Wilford C. Wood of Bountiful, Utah.[4] These volumes are available today.

There have been several revisions of the original Book of Mormon. A number of revisions have been made down through the years of time resulting in our present Book of Mormon. An examination of the photo reprint of the original edition of the Book of Mormon as compared with our present edition shows that there have been over 4000 changes made. This is between just two copies. The New Testament has about twenty significant textual problems. Between the early Book of Mormon and the pre-

---

[3] The evidence for biblical accuracy has been briefly outlined in Chapter One, pages 5-12. The evidence shows that the Bible has come down to us today substantially unchanged and remarkably accurate. A vast library of evidence is available to document this remarkable preservation of these ancient documents.

[4] Available from Modern Microfilm, 1350 S. West Temple, Salt Lake City, UT 81501.

sent Book of Mormon, there have been over 4000 textual problems. These problems are a part of the very fabric, the warp and woof, of the text. These problems consist of poor grammar, poor English, mispronounced words, and historical and geographical errors that run throughout the text.

To summarize, there can be no doubt as to what was said in the original, yet the closer we get to the original document the more filled with error it becomes. It is exactly the opposite of what is found in an examination of the Bible text.

ARCHAEOLOGY AS PROOF OF THE BIBLE AND BOOK OF MORMON

Archaeology as Proof of the Bible

Does archaeology prove the accuracy of the Bible? The Bible has been carefully examined as to its archaeological evidence. A general rule is that if the Bible says it, you can find it. One of the oldest cities mentioned in the Bible, that has been found, is Ur of the Chaldees.[5,6] This city had many modern conveniences, and yes, it was called Ur just like the Bible said.

The Bible talks about the cities of Sodom and Gommorah. These cities were, for many years, a subject of heated discussion as to whether they really existed or not. Just two years ago, archaeologists uncovered the five cities of the plains mentioned in the book of Genesis, chapter 14. The remains of Sodom and Gommorah are thought to have been found and were burned just as the Bible said.[7]

In recent excavations at Ebla, Syria, bills of lading were found from shipments made to the cities of Sodom and Gommorah.

The city of Jericho has been found just as it was said to have been in the book of Joshua. The cities of Hazor, Megiddo, Bethel and Jerusalem have also been found, with many others.

If the Bible mentions it, you can find it is the usual rule. Ancient nations are mentioned such as Babylonia and Assyria, with

---

[5] Genesis 11:28.

[6] Further research can be done by reading *Everyday Life in Bible Times* (National Geographic Society, Washington, D.C., 1967).

[7] *Biblical Archaeology Review*, Sept-Oct. 1980, p. 26.

the capitals Babylon and Nineveh. These have been found and excavated.

One can get a fresh drink of water from the Gihon spring that is mentioned a number of times in our Bible. The Gihon spring is the place where King Solomon was annointed king. It was the route of entrance of David and his soldiers into the city of Jebush to conquer Jerusalem. By entering the tunnel to the city, he captured Jerusalem and made it his capital. The Gihon spring is a place that Jesus and the apostles would have gone for a drink of fresh water while they were in Jerusalem. It was Jerusalem's only fresh water supply in Bible times.

If the Bible says it, you can find it. The period of history that is covered goes back about 4000 years. This is ancient history.

Archaeology and the Book of Mormon

The archaeology of the Book of Mormon is of a much, much more recent period of history. Instead of going back 4000 or more years, the period covered goes back about 2500 years. It is what could be called relatively modern history. Yet, not one city as named in the Book of Mormon has ever been found—not one.

The information of an archaeological nature, that is found in the Book of Mormon, was well known in the days of Joseph Smith, the days of the writing of the Book of Mormon.[8] Can we substantiate the Book of Mormon archaeologically? No! Yet this is a modern period of history, in what is a well populated land today, North and South America. Where is the land of Zarahemla ever heard of outside the Book of Mormon? Where is the valley of Nimrod? Where are the plains of Nephihah? There is a little rule that seems fitting: if the Book of Mormon says it, you can count on not finding it, as named.

REAL PEOPLE AS PROOF OF THE BIBLE AND THE BOOK OF MORMON

People of the Bible

The people mentioned in the Bible, such as Abraham, Nahor,

---

[8] Larry Jonas, *Mormon Claims Examined* (Grand Rapids, MI: Baker Book House, 1961), pp. 21-48 gives a clear indication that the archaeological evidence in the Book of Mormon was well known in the days that the Book of Mormon was first published.

Moses, Saul, David, Solomon, Jesus, Paul, and Peter, are almost household words throughout America today. There is literally tons of evidence, outside the Bible, that these people lived. They lived during a period of time 2000-4000 years ago. This is ancient history and extends to a period of relatively modern history.

People of the Book of Mormon

In the Book of Mormon such people are named as Nephi, Laman, Lehi, Joneam, Zenos, Zerahemnah, and Zorum. Outside the Book of Mormon we have absolutely no evidence that these people ever lived. They fit into a much more recent period of history than our Bible.

NUMISTOLOGY–THE BIBLE AND THE BOOK OF MORMON

The Bible

What does the study of numistology show us about the Bible? The Bible mentions a number of different coins, such as the shekel, which was a silver coin, or the half-shekel, half of the value of the shekel. The Bible also mentions the mite (Mark 12:42). Drams were gold coins. The denarius and the copper penny are spoken of in Matthew 18:28. When the Bible tells of it, you can be sure it existed and can be found.[9]

To give you an indication of the availability of these coins, the author has a silver shekel, possibly from the period of Augustus Caesar, in his coin collection. It is an authentic, real shekel like the Bible mentions from the time of Christ. The Bible is a real record of real events. In this collection is also a first century mite, like the widow gave at the temple in Jerusalem. The money of the Bible is still available today.

The Book of Mormon and Numistology

The Book of Mormon, in Alma 11:5-19, gives the following list of coins. There is the senine of gold, the seon of gold, shum of gold and limnah of gold. It tells of silver coins, the senum of silver, am-

---

[9] If you want to check further information about these coins, I would suggest looking in *Unger's Bible Dictionary*, pages 723-726.

nor of silver, the ezron of silver and the omti of silver. It then lists the lesser coins: the shiblon, the shiblum, and the leah. Need it be said at this point not one of these coins has ever been found?

Another important question is, why did these Jews who left the Middle East and came to America change the names of their money so drastically? Why have none of them ever been found as named? Numistology demonstrates that the Book of Mormon is not a real story but a fairy tale.

THE BIBLE AND SCIENCE – THE BOOK OF MORMON AND SCIENCE

The Bible

A good test for the Bible is, is it scientifically and medically accurate? The Bible mentions a lot about science and a lot about medicine, although it is not a scientific or medical book. The Bible says that "Life is in the blood of man," in Leviticus 17:11-14. This is medically true. The Bible gives laws of sanitation in Deuteronomy 23:12-13, that will purify even the most stubborn of modern infections, such as staph infection. The sanitary code of the book of Deuteronomy is so perfect that it has been little improved on in all the succeeding centuries of time. It is remarkable evidence of the inspiration of our Bible.[10]

The Bible speaks of rivers in the sea (Psalms 8:8). Modern oceanography has established the accuracy of this statement. The Bible speaks of the earth being round (Isaiah 40:22). This has been proved true with our space travel of today. The Bible tells us that the moon has no light of itself (Job 25:5). This, too, has been found to be true. The Bible long before the advent of our modern telescopes said that the north was empty of stars (Job 26:7). This, too, has been proven to be true. The tabernacle of the Old Testament, built by Moses, was of such a perfect nature that it could be pitched on sand and not settle or move. A man seeking a modern patent on a similar type of tent found that he had been preceded by

---

[10] For further information about this subject, read *None of These Diseases.* It is written by Dr. S. I. McMillan, M.D. This book is a Spire Book and indicates how wonderfully intricate and complete was the sanitary code of the Old Testament.

3500 years. The Bible is always accurate when it speaks about science or medicine.

The Book of Mormon

Do we find the same thing true with the Book of Mormon? Let's observe only a very brief sampling of what is found. The Book of Mormon speaks of spring steel (1 Nephi 16:18), 592 years before the time of Christ.[11] What does it take to make spring steel? First of all, a craftsman needs iron ore, coal, and limestone. After mining the ore, coal and limestone, he would need a blast furnace. When he has finished the blast furnace process, he would need semi-finishing mills, and finishing mills. Is it really likely that they had spring steel?

The *World Book Encyclopedia* says some steel was made in very small quantities, as early as a little bit before the birth of Christ. It wasn't until 1722 that a French physicist learned how to make steel in large quantities. Steel was not made in America until 1832. Modern research gives us good reason to question the statements of spring steel in 1 Nephi 16:18.

The Book of Mormon refers to electricity in 1 Nephi 17:53. This was 591 years before Christ. Serious questions need to be asked about the scientific accuracy of the Book of Mormon.

The Book of Mormon speaks of the compass in 1 Nephi 18:12, 590 B.C. The list of scientific inaccuracies could go on and on. The book is not scientifically accurate. The textual critic immediately knows that a book that claims to be ancient is not ancient if it mentions modern inventions.

THE BIBLE AND BOOK OF MORMON AND PROPHECY

The Bible

The text of Scripture has within it many hundreds, possibly even thousands, of prophecies. These prophecies are found in both the Old Testament and New Testament alike. There are over 330 prophecies about Christ found in the Old Testament.

---

[11] Four times the word steel is used in the King James Version of the Bible, 2 Sam. 22:35; Job 20-24; Psalms 18:34 and Jer. 15:12. The Hebrew word is not steel but the word Nihash or bronze. Again we have a case of poor King James Translation leading to an incorrect understanding.

A few examples will help illustrate our point. Isaiah 7:14, NASV says:

> Therefore the Lord himself will give you a sign; Behold, a virgin shall conceive, and bear a son, and shall call His name Immanuel.

Isaiah 9:6-7, NASV says:

> For a child will be born to us, a son will be given to us; and the government will rest on His shoulders; And His name will be called Wonderful Counselor, Mighty God, Eternal Father, Prince of Peace. There will be no end to the increase of His government or of peace, On the throne of David and over his kingdom, To establish it and to uphold it with justice and righteousness From then on and forevermore. The zeal of the Lord of hosts will accomplish this.

Isaiah 53:3-6 gives quite a detailed prophecy about Christ. This prophecy says:

> He was despised and forsaken of men, A man of sorrows, and acquainted with grief; And like one from whom men hide their face, He was despised, and we did not esteem Him. Surely our griefs He Himself bore, And our sorrows He carried; Yet we ourselves esteemed Him stricken, Smitten of God, and afflicted. But He was pierced through for our transgressions, He was crushed for our iniquities; The chastening for our well-being fell upon Him, And by His scourging we are healed. All of us like sheep have gone astray, Each of us has turned to his own way; But the Lord has caused the iniquity of us all to fall on Him. (NASV)

There is something that can be observed about these prophecies about Christ. They are not clear enough that a person could have fulfilled them intentionally at a later date. Rather, they speak in guarded terms, in somewhat symbolic language. After looking back at them, when the prophecy has been fulfilled, it is very clear that they were prophecies and that these prophecies were fulfilled. Yet, there is always a certain ambiguity about Old Testament prophecy that leaves it rather obscure. The prophetic writer himself often did not understand what he was speaking about until after the event had been fulfilled. This is a rule that is true of all Old Testament prophecies.

A close look at the Bible manuscripts, particularly the Dead Sea Scrolls, will show that these prophecies were prophecies. We have copies of the Old Testament dating from 125 to 225 B.C. This shows for sure that they were prophecies. They were given hundreds of years in advance of the events.

The Book of Mormon

In the Book of Mormon there are fantastic prophecies. But here is where the problem lies. They tell too much, they say too much. For example, Jacob 6:6-9 says:

> Yea, today, if ye will hear his voice, harden not your hearts; for why will ye die? For behold, after ye have been nourished by the good word of God all the day long, will ye bring forth evil fruit, that ye must be hewn down and cast into the fire? Behold, will ye reject these words? Will ye reject the words of the prophets; and will ye reject all the words which have been spoken concerning Christ, after so many have spoken concerning Him; and deny the good word of Christ, and the power of God, and the gift of the Holy Ghost, and quench the Holy Spirit, and make a mock of the great plan of redemption, which hath been laid for you? Know ye not that if ye will do these things, that the power of the redemption and the resurrection, which is in Christ, will bring you to stand with shame and awful guilt before the bar of God?

This particular prophecy was given about fifty or thirty years before the time of Christ. Isn't it remarkable that many of the main details of the life of Christ, including his name, his resurrection, the Holy Spirit, and redemption are mentioned in this one brief passage? It leads one to believe, in comparing it with the Bible, that this was a prophecy written after the event, not before, as is claimed. It is very easy to prophecy after the fact. Only God knows the good future.

Whenever a prophecy is too detailed, names are given and all the details about the life of the person and events to come are given, then it is wise to be suspicious of that prophecy. This elaborate and detailed type of prophecy is given on and off throughout the Book of Mormon. Such things as baptism and remission of sins being preached in the days of Christ are often spoken of. This is serious textual evidence showing that the Book of Mormon really is not a book of prophecy at all as claimed. It is prophecy written after the event.

These prophecies bear too much resemblance to the terminology and language of the King James version. We thus are able to trace them to their real source which was in fact a quotation from the King James version of the Bible. They were put into the Book of Mormon framework to appear as prophecy.

If the Book of Mormon is true, then certainly the words of Ephesians 3:8-10 are not true:

> To me, the very least of all saints, this grace was given, to preach to the Gentiles the unfathomable riches of Christ, and to bring to light what is the

administration of the mystery which for ages has been hidden in God, who created all things; in order that the manifold wisdom of God might now be made known through the church to the rulers and the authorities in the heavenly places. (NASV)

If the Book of Mormon is true, then the Bible is not true, because the Bible makes it very clear that these mysteries had been hidden in ages past.

AUTHOR'S STYLE OF WRITING

An author's style of writing is almost as distinctive as is his handwriting. The textual critic seeks to determine how many authors were involved in producing an ancient manuscript.

The Bible

The Bible has many different authors; the style of writing is as varied as Moses, Amos, Paul and Peter. A cursory thumbing through shows the obviously different styles of the numerous authors. Over forty different authors and styles of writing have been verified in our Bible.

Such things as vocabulary, phrases, sentence structure, length or shortness of sentences make up an author's distinctive style.

The Book of Mormon

A text critical study of the Book of Mormon shows a similar style of writing from beginning to end. There are a number of distinctive fingerprints of the author throughout.

The only exception to this rule is in the places the Book of Mormon quotes the Bible. Here varied styles of writing suddenly burst upon the textual critic.

There are some obvious indications that the Book of Mormon was not written by many different prophets who engraved them on brass plates and left them for posterity. The evidence points to a one man authorship.

The first and most obvious is the continual use of the phrase "and it came to pass." This phrase is used many times in the King James version of the Bible. This represents a very poor transla-

tion of the Hebrew verb *hayah* with its variations.[12]

The Book of Mormon is filled with the phrase "and it came to pass...." Below is a tabulation.[13]

I Nephi	179	
II Nephi	23	(quotes the Book of Isaiah extensively—never found in a biblical quote.)
Jacob	42	
Enos	5	short books
Jarom	4	short books
Omni	10	short books
Words of Mormon	2	short books
Mosiah	155	
Alma	351	
Helaman	110	
III Nephi	124	
IV Nephi	19	
Mormon	15	
Ether	133	
Moroni	0	
Total	1212	

Without a doubt this can be called a distinctive mannerism of an author. It is found in all but one book. Since the book claims to have been written by numerous authors we can hardly accept it as an authentic record.

Other textual items that show each book to have the same authorship are: 1. Long involved sentences; 2. Same vocabulary; 3

[12] The King James Version's indiscriminate translation of the many variations of the Hebrew verb *hayah* into "And it came to pass" or "It came to pass" amounts to a very poor, unimaginative translation of its near fifty possibilities and robs the translation of clearer meaning. This style is copied by the Book of Mormon writer to make his work sound like the Bible. This plagerism of the King James style and in one of its very poorest translations shows the Book of Mormon not to be of God. A proper translation of the Hebrew would render very few of these "And it came to pass" instances.

The New Testament King James Version translates *kai egeneto* "And it came to pass." This phenomenon is found in four New Testament books, the synoptic gospels and Acts. Mark was likely written first. Matthew and Luke used Mark as a source for their gospels and thus the "And it came to pass" terminology. Luke wrote Acts and used this familiar style. Here again a careful translation renders few of these passages, "And it came to pass."

The Book of Mormon is caught plagerizing the poor translation style of the King James Version to appear to be what it really isn't, scripture. (For this reason the author strongly suggests the use of a better translation, the New American Standard Version.)

[13] Author's own count. It is possible many "it came to passes" could have been missed.

Outlandish distinctive names, many nowhere else ever heard of before; 4. Similar plot with little variation from beginning to end; 5. Similar prophetic message, the coming messiah, yet always in very similar words; 6. Most of the books quote the King James Version of the Bible; 7. Poor grammar and English usage thoroughout. Only one conclusion can be reached. The Book of Mormon was written by one author.

REAL STORIES OF REAL EVENTS

The Bible

Archaeology has been about proving the Bible for well over a century. Under careful scrutiny the Bible stories have been vindicated time after time. It is true that many Bible stories cannot be checked. Yet, each has within it the seeds of truth. Miracles do abound and were no embarrassment to Jesus or His Apostles. From beginning to end, it bears the marks of credibility. Even such stories as Sodom and Gomorrah have been proven true.

The Book of Mormon

1. Nephi's sword factory, temple, kingship, and the Lamanite curse.

The people who left Jerusalem and who are the basis of the Mormon history numbered about fifteen to twenty. They were: (1) Lehi; (2) his wife Sariah; (3) Laman; (4) Lemuel; (5) Sam; (6) Nephi; (7-8) daughters of Ishael (two) (9)Ishael; (10-15) two sons of Ishael - their families; (16-17) Jacob and Joseph born 590 B.C. The church office of the Utah branch church estimates their number to be about fifteen souls plus two boys born in the wilderness. (18) Zoram somewhere enters the story. II Nephi 5:6.

In II Nephi 5:6 the group separates. Nephi takes with him - (1) Nephi; (2) Zoram; (3) Sam; (4-5) Jacob and Joseph, now 20 years old and (6-8) the women. This makes their number three men and two boys and three women.

At this point let us take up the story. II Nephi 5:14-16,18, 21-22.

> And I, Nephi, did take the sword of Laban, and after the manner of it did make many swords, lest by any means the people who were now called Lamanites should come upon us and destroy us; for I knew their hatred towards me and my children and those who were called my people. 15. And I

did teach my people to build buildings, and to work in all manner of wood, and of iron, and of copper, and of brass, and of steel, and of gold, and of silver, and of precious ores, which were in great abundance. 16. And I, Nephi, did build a temple; and I did construct it after the manner of the temple of Solomon save it were not built of so many precious things; for they were not to be found upon the land; wherefore, it could not be built like unto Solomon's temple. But the manner of the construction was like unto the temple of Solomon; and the workmanship thereof was exceeding fine.... 18. And it came to pass that they would that I should be their king. But I, Nephi, was desirous that they should have no king; nevertheless, I did for them according to that which was in my power.... (Of the Lamanites it was said) 21. ...the Lord God did cause a skin of blackness to come upon them. 22. And thus saith the Lord God: I will cause that they shall be loathsome unto thy people, save they shall repent of their iniquities.

The sword of Laban was used as a pattern to make swords. Remember, there were three men. What does it take to make swords? Ore deposits, mining, transporting, smelting, fluxing, forming, grinding, assembling. Does it sound plausible for three men who are providing for their families in the wilderness to have a sword factory?

Next, we have added to this story carpentry, iron working, copper, brass, steel, gold, silver and precious ores. Three men doing all these things? Did they have all these mines, all these refining processes? Did they have a steel mill? *The World Book Encyclopedia* says steel was not made in America until 1832.[14] Anyway, where would three men get a blast furnace?

The third problem has to do with building a temple like Solomon's. His took 170,000 men seven years to build.[15] It cost five to ten billion dollars. Are we to suppose that these men built such a structure at all, let alone in two to ten years?

The fourth problem is the obvious contradiction. Verse fifteen says all of the ingredients found in Solomon's temple were in great abundance. Verse sixteen says they could not be found in the land. Which is the truth of the matter?

The next problem is why would six to ten people need to elect a king, as stated in verse eighteen?

---

14 *The World Book Encyclopedia*, volume 10 (Chicago, IL 1964), pp. 356-360.

15 I Kings 6:38; I Kings 5:13-18

Finally, who could believe that people's skin color had anything to do with their godliness or lack of godliness? See vs. 21-22.

Could you believe this scripture, or would it be more fitting to believe it is a fairy tale like *Alice in Wonderland*?

2. Cowboy snakes.

In Ether 9:26-29 we find the following story:

> And the people had spread again over all the face of the land, and there began again to be an exceeding great wickedness upon the face of the land, and Heth began to embrace the secret plans again of old, to destroy his father.... 29. But the people believed not the words of the prophets, but they cast them out;.... 30. And it came to pass that there began to be a great dearth upon the land, and the inhabitants began to be destroyed exceeding fast because of the dearth for there was no rain upon the face of the earth. 31. And there came forth poisonous serpents also upon the face of the land, and did poison many people. And it came to pass that their flocks began to flee before the poisonous serpents, towards the land southward, which was called by the Nephites Zarahemla. 32. And it came to pass that there were many of them which did perish by the way; nevertheless, there were some which fled into the land southward. 33. And it came to pass that the Lord did cause the serpents that they should pursue them no more, but that they should hedge up the way that the people could not pass.... 34. And it came to pass that the people did follow the course of the beasts, and did devour the carcasses of them which fell by the way....

Exactly where the land of Zarahemla is no one knows. Some have supposed it was in the Isthmus of Panama area. Can you imagine snakes on a cattle drive, humping along behind loping cattle? Can you imagine the snakes setting up guards to keep the people and cattle apart? Can you imagine people eating the poisoned cattle?

Is this a real story or a fairy tale? Doesn't it seem more reasonable to believe it is a fairy tale?

There are literally dozens of such fantastic, unbelievable stories in the Book of Mormon. Scripture? No! Fairy tale? Yes!

OTHER PROBLEMS WITH THE BOOK OF MORMON

The Book of Mormon Quotes Extensively from the Bible

This would be fine, except it always quotes from the King James Version, which was not translated for 1190 years after the Book of Mormon was finished.

There is a rule of textual criticism. If a supposed ancient book quotes from a modern book then the book is not ancient. There are two possibilities. The Bible quotes the Book of Mormon. This is impossible, as Bible writers did not have the Book of Mormon in their possession. The King James translators did not. Or, the Book of Mormon quotes from the Bible. This is the only possible alternative.

The Book of Mormon is thus demonstrated to be a relatively modern book written after 1611 A.D.

Where Did the Book of Mormon Come From?[16]

Conclusive evidence indicates that it was written by a Congregational preacher Solomon Spaulding, about 1810. He called his book *Manuscript Found.*

This book was probably stolen by Sidney Rigdon from Patterson's Print Shop, of Pittsburg, Penn. He and Joseph Smith conspired to publish it as a book from God.

The evidence for his having written the book is as follows:

1. Eight people who read both books testified under oath that they were the same. They were John Spaulding, Martha Spaulding, John Miller, Henry Lake, Artemas Cunningham, Aaron Wright, Nahum Howard and Matilda (Spaulding) Davidson, Solomon Spaulding's widow.[17]

2. When the Book of Mormon was being first published several pages of the original handwritten manuscript were lost at the printers. Joseph Smith rushed home and came back with the missing pages. These are a part of the handwritten original document owned by the L.D.S. Church. These pages are in Solomon Spaulding's own handwriting. He was already dead when the Book of Mormon was supposedly translated.

MORMON NAMES - ORIGINS

A. Nephi - comes from 2 Maccabbees 1:36
B. Lehi - a Hebrew word meaning "jawbone of an ass"
C. Mormon - A classical Greek word - one meaning is monster
D. Moroni - Moron with an "i" added

---

16 Cowdry, Davis and Scales, *Who Really Wrote the Book of Mormon?* (Vision House Publishers, Santa Anna, CA 1977).

17 *Ibid.*, pp.32-46.

E. Amaron
F. Amlicites
G. Helaman
H. Mosiah
I. Enos
J. Jerom
K. Omni

The singularly different names and words are found throughout the book. Some have meaning. Some are the product of the writer's own fertile imagination.

Spaulding was an avid reader. He had a consuming interest in Indian folklore and archaeology. He had a masters degree.[18] He was a preacher and familiar with the King James Bible. This amply supplied him with the sources he needed to write this book.

It was only left to the devices of a scheming man and his friend to publish it as scripture and to present it to an unsuspecting public.

THE BIBLE STANDS THE TEST
THE BOOK OF MORMON HAS FAILED IT

The Bible is an actual record of real events. The Book of Mormon is a fairy tale, the product of the writer's fertile imagination. What holds the spell upon Mormon people that they do not readily see the error of this book? It is almost like a snake charming a bird.[19]

The author's prayer is that deluded people might believe the Bible, God's word to man, and be made aware of blind guides, such as the Book of Mormon.

Chapter IV

MORMON THEOLOGY AND THE BOOK OF MORMON

The Mormon Church of today does not go by the Book of Mormon. Many clear teachings of the Book of Mormon are ignored as

---

18 *Ibid.*, pg. 29.

19 II Corinthians 4:3-4.

unimportant. This is hard to understand since the Mormon people claim such allegiance to it as a direct revelation from God. Here are several illustrations to show their departure from its teachings.

Baptism For The Dead

One of the cardinal doctrines of the Latter-day Saints is baptism for the dead. One will not study with them very long before the subject will come up. Much of their temple work centers around this matter of getting the unbaptized dead, baptized. Yet it is strange that the Book of Mormon teaches that once a man has died without being saved, he is sealed to Satan forever. Notice what Alma has to say on the subject.

> For behold, this life is the time for men to prepare to meet God; yea, behold the day of this life is the day for men to perform their labors. And now, as I said unto you before, as ye have had so many witnesses, therefore, I beseech of you that ye do not procrastinate the day of your repentance until the end; for after this day of life, which is given us to prepare for eternity, behold, if we do not improve our time while in this life, which is given us to prepare for eternity, behold, if we do not improve our time while in this life, then cometh the night of darkness wherein there can be no labor performed. Ye cannot say, when ye are brought to that awful crisis, that I will repent, that I will return to my God. Nay, ye cannot say this; for that same spirit which doth possess your bodies at the time that ye go out of this life, that same spirit will have power to possess your body in that eternal world. For behold, if ye have procrastinated the day of your repentance even until death, behold, ye have become subjected to the spirit of the devil, and he doth seal you his; therefore, the Spirit of the Lord hath withdrawn from you, and hath no place in you, and the devil hath all power over you; and this is the final state of the wicked.[1]

Such plain language is hard to misunderstand. The excuse that is often given when this passage is shown to Mormon leaders is that God makes mistakes and has to constantly upgrade his doctrine to remove such errors. How can we know what is truth and what is not, if God is so untrustworthy?

There is a more complete discussion of baptism for the dead in Part IV.

God Has A Body of Parts and Passions

Another doctrine of the Latter-day Saints is that God is a God

---

1 The Book of Mormon, Alma 34:32-35.

of body, parts, and passion. Mormon theology pictures God as an exalted man who has gotten ahead of us in what is called eternal progression. Their teaching goes so far as to suggest that Jesus was begotten by God, physically, having relations with Mary. Part IV will discuss God being a spirit and the subject of the virgin birth. Their doctrines will be quoted at that time. At the present, observe that the Book of Mormon teaches the same doctrine about God that the Bible does. That is, that God is spirit.

> And the king said: Is God that Great Spirit that brought our fathers out of the land of Jerusalem? And Aaron said unto him: Yea, he is that Great Spirit, and he created all things both in heaven and in earth. Believest thou this? And he said: Yea, I believe that the Great Spirit created all things, and I desire that ye should tell me concerning all these things, and I will believe thy words.[2]

When we consider the Mormon doctrine of eternal progression, that God is growing and becoming wiser and stronger, the Book of Mormon says:

> For do we not read that God is the same yesterday, today, and forever, and in him there is no variableness neither shadow of changing? And now if ye have imagined up unto yourselves a god who doth vary, and in whom there is shadow of changing, then have ye imagined up unto yourselves a god who is not a God of miracles. But behold, I will show unto you a God of miracles, even the God of Abraham, and the God of Isaac, and the God of Jacob; and it is the same God who created the heavens and the earth and all things that in them are.[3]

Moroni says about the same thing. "For I know that God is not a partial God, neither a changeable being; but he is unchangeable from all eternity to all eternity."[4] These statements are opposed to the current doctrine of the Mormon Church. The Mormon Church does not go by the Book of Mormon.

Another doctrine that is currently taught by the Latter-day Saints, which is not taught in the Bible, is that man can be exalted to being a God. The Book of Mormon repeatedly states that there is only one true God.

> Now Zeezrom saith again unto him: Is the Son of God the very Eternal Father? And Amulek said unto him: Yes, he is the very Eternal Father of

---

2 *Ibid.*, 22:9-11.

3 The Book of Mormon, Mormon 9:9-11

4 The Book of Mormon, Moroni 8:18.

heaven and of earth, and all things which in them are; he is the beginning and the end, the first and the last.[5]

Neither the Mormon Church, nor the Bible, affirms that Jesus and the Father are one and the same; but beyond this fact, we find here a statement that God the Father is the beginning and end of all things. This does not sound like other Gods, or that man may become God.

These doctrinal issues about God, Christ, eternal progression, and baptism for the dead will be considered more fully in Part IV.

Why Criticize The Bible?

Another perplexing passage is, "Thou fool, that shall say: A Bible, we have got a Bible, and we need no more Bible."[6] What good can be accomplished by indicating that the Bible is incomplete? Why call a person a fool that would want to hold to the Bible?

Poor Grammar

In many places the grammar is quite poor in the Book of Mormon. Here are a few examples. In II Nephi we find, "...many of which sayings are written upon mine other plates; for a more history part are written upon mine other plates."[7] Or, "O Lord wilt thou not shut the gates of thy righteous before me, that I may walk in the path of the low valley, that I may be strict in the plain road,"[8] and again, "and the stiffneckedness of men."[9] This type of poor sentence structure and grammar can be found throughout the book.

Contradictions Between The Book of Mormon And The Doctrine and Covenants

One simple rule, dictated by common sense, is that truth does not contradict itself. If God cannot lie, and he cannot, then one would expect His revelations to be consistent throughout.

---

5 The Book of Mormon, Alma 11:38-39.

6 The Book of Mormon, II Nephi 29:6.

7 *Ibid.*, 4:14.

8 *Ibid.*, 4:32.

9 *Ibid.*, 32:7.

Something can't be bad and good at the same time. Yet, examination shows that the Book of Mormon and the Doctrine and Covenants definitely contradict each other. About the matter of polygamy, it is recorded in the Book of Mormon:

> And now it came to pass that the people of Nephi, under the reign of the second king, began to grow hard in their hearts, and indulge themselves somewhat in wicked practices, such as like unto David of old desiring many wives and concubines, and also Solomon, his son.[10]
>
> Behold, David and Solomon truly had many wives and concubines, which thing was abominable before me, saith the Lord. ...Wherefore, I the Lord God will not suffer that this people shall do like unto them of old. Wherefore, my brethren, hear me, and hearken to the word of the Lord: For there shall not any man among you have save it be one wife, and concubines he shall have none.[11]

Yet when we turn to the Doctrine and Covenants we find an entirely different view of the matter, for it says:

> David also received many wives and concubines, and also Solomon and Moses my servants, as also many others of my servants, from the beginning of creation until this time; and in nothing did they sin save in those things which they received not of me. David's wives and concubines were given unto him of me, by the hand of Nathan, my servant, and others of the prophets who had the keys of this power; and in none of these things did he sin against me....[12]

How can a man be both condemned and justified for the same act? This is a sure, open contradiction. Apparently one or both records are not of God.

So in conclusion, since the Book of Mormon has had to be changed so many times to make it correct, yet claims to be translated by a prophet with God's help, it is difficult to accept it as scripture. Because the book contains so many textual problems, modern words, quotations from modern literature, poor logic, uncertain prophets, modern scientific terminology, ridiculously absurd stories, theology contrary to that of the current prophet, poor grammar, and contradictions between it and later supposed revelations, we must reject it as scripture. A world of difference separates it from the Bible.

---

12 Doctrine and Covenants 132:38-39.

10 The Book of Mormon, Jacob 1:15.

11 *Ibid.*, 2:24-27.

Chapter V

THE DOCTRINE AND COVENANTS

The Doctrine and Covenants is a series of revelations, supposedly given to Joseph Smith, with minor additions by later successors in the presidency of the Latter-day Saints.

The first revelation, according to his testimony, was given to Joseph Smith in September of 1823 and he received the last in June of 1844. There is one section given by Brigham Young, and short notes by Presidents Wilford Woodruff and Lorenzo Snow.

For the most part the Doctrine and Covenants is the work of Joseph Smith. The Doctrine and Covenants introduces many of the different doctrinal ideas that were taught by the Mormon Church. It is the Doctrine and Covenants that makes the Mormon church so different from most other religious bodies in America. The serious theological problems come from this book. The Doctrine and Covenants is much more difficult for Latter-day Saints to defend than the Book of Mormon. While the Book of Mormon is a book about the size of our Old Testament, the Doctrine and Covenants is about the size of the New Testament.

An original edition of the Doctrine and Covenants is available through the means of photo reprint. It is printed by the Mormon Church in Salt Lake City, Utah. It is called, *Joseph Smith Begins His Work II* and is a companion volume to the photo reprint of the Book of Mormon. Wilford C. Wood also published this volume through the agency of the Deseret News Publishing Company, the official printing organ of the Mormon Church. This volume bears a sworn and notarized statement by Wilford C. Wood and The Deseret News Publishing Company indicating that this is an authentic photo copy of the original Book of Commandments, now called the Doctrine and Covenants. There is no room for doubt that this is authentic. It is readily accepted by Mormon Church leaders.

The original Doctrine and Covenants (Book of Commandments) was published in 1833.

The very first section of the Doctrine and Covenants tells us that these revelations are from God.

What I the Lord have spoken, I have spoken, and I excuse not myself; and though the heavens and the earth pass away, my word shall not pass away, but shall all be fulfilled, whether by mine own voice or by the voice of my servants, it is the same. For behold, and lo, the Lord is God, and the Spirit beareth record, and the record is true, and the truth abideth forever and ever. Amen.[1]

After this affirmation one is shocked to learn that the Doctrine and Covenants has been greatly edited and changed. In fact, there are over 2,786 changes. These are not changes of minor significance, but of major importance. By what justification could someone, Joseph Smith or anyone else, take out whole paragraphs, put in whole paragraphs, reverse the meaning, contradict what was originally said, when in no uncertain language Section One says these words would never pass away? If the original revelations were true, and the truth abides forever, why then would they have to be rewritten, revised, reversed, and changed?

Now, if in truth these were revelations from God, like the Bible, why would any man want to correct what God had given. For a man to take in hand to change these commands, without telling the reader why or when he had done so, seems unthinkable, unless they weren't really revelations from God in the first place, especially in the light of Section One which clearly affirms that these are God's words and that they will never pass away.

Pages 35-48 of this book are photo copies of the original Doctrine and Covenants (Book of Commandments) with the changes marked to show how the present Doctrine and Covenants reads.[2] Remember that these are supposed revelations from God above, recorded by His "prophet." Remember too, as you look at these pages, that Section One says these words would never pass away, that they were all true and would stand forever.

This is very damaging evidence. It is inconceivable that this is the work of the God of the universe. We have already learned that the Bible has not gone through much mutilation. In fact, the men given charge of the Bible protected it most carefully lest they would lose the very words of God.

---

[1] Doctrine and Covenants 1:38-39.

[2] These pages are used by permission of Jerald Tanner and Sandra Tanner and are photo copies of pages 18-24 in their book, *Mormonism—Shadow or Reality?*, enl. ed. (Salt Lake City, Utah: Modern Microfilm, 1972).

An explanation of the changes is likely necessary. The printed portion of the photo copies is the original Book of Commandments, now called the Doctrine and Covenants. The margin is marked to show how the present Doctrine and Covenants reads. Letters are used to indicate what type of change is made. T.C. means textual change. W.A. means words added. W.D. means words deleted. In the margin are large printed letters: A, B, C, and so forth. These indicate doctrinal changes. A brief explanation for some of these changes and their significance is in order. Some of the changes that involve the fewest words are the most serious.

The first change, marked "A" on page 40, is a serious change. If you will read carefully you will notice that originally Joseph Smith is told that he will have no other work from God than the translation of the plates into the English Book of Mormon. He is to pretend to have no other work from God. Then a few years later he decided that this wasn't enough, God supposedly changed His mind. It was changed so that he could have further revelations from God. We are forced into one of two conclusions: either God changed His mind, didn't think ahead sufficiently, made a mistake, or Joseph Smith wrote the revelation and when he found out how well the people received his first work, The Book of Mormon, decided that he had limited himself too much by saying he would get no further revelation, so changed it so he could get more. Either way we must realize that this cannot be a revelation from the God of the universe.

Under change "C," on page 41, we see that the original teaches that the church was to be built up like the church of old, the New Testament church. When, later, Joseph Smith wanted to change some things in the church from the original design, they had to change the Doctrine and Covenants. So they removed 154 words by the stroke of a pen. What had been claimed to be a revelation from Almighty God has now been removed. Are we to believe that it really was a revelation from God?

Under change "D" we find a document supposedly translated from some parchments written by John the Apostle, later found and translated by Joseph Smith. In a book by Jerald Tanner we read:

This revelation is supposed to contain a translation of a parchment written by the Apostle John. Joseph Smith was supposed to have translated it by means of the Urim and Thummim. When this revelation was published in the Book of Commandments in 1833, it contained 143 words, but when it was reprinted in the Doctrine and Covenants in 1835, it contained 252 words. Thus 109 words had been added.[3]

Several explanations could be given for such changes. All of them boil down to the fact that the "revelations" have been very carelessly handled, changed, and revised at the will of those who received them. We can only conclude that those who claimed to be from God were not trustworthy people.

To think that one would, without explanation, add to the letter of another is unthinkable unless the person doing the adding was not honest. This is good evidence that Joseph Smith was not a prophet of God.

Change "H," on page 45, is of significance since it makes way for changing the church and its doctrine. Originally they were told to build upon the things which were already written. "For in them are all things written concerning my church, my gospel, and my rock."[4] When Joseph Smith wanted to change things later he had to change this. So, by adding just a few words, he made way for changing the Church of the Lord. It was made to read, "For in them are all things written concerning the foundation of my church, my gospel, and my rock."[5] By adding three words he made way to change the church as he wished.

Change "J," on page 49 represents only one word, but it is a serious doctrinal change. Originally Joseph Smith supported his family "from" the church. Later when he wanted to do away with people getting salaries from the church, thus making a way for the church to grow great financially, the word was changed from "from" to "in." This changes the whole meaning and thus introduces a whole new doctrine. This is further proof that this is not a revelation from God.

Change "L," on page 51, is a serious change of teaching. Originally the teaching was: "...and behold, thou shalt consecrate all thy properties, that which thou hast unto me, with a covenant

---

[3] Jerald Tanner and Sandra Tanner, *Mormonism—Shadow or Reality?*, enl. ed. (Salt Lake City, Utah: Modern Microfilm, 1972), p. 27.

[4] Book of Commandments 15:3.

[5] Doctrine and Covenants 18:4.

BOOK OF COMMANDMENTS - Chapter 4
COMPARE DOCTRINE AND COVENANTS - Sec. 5:1-11

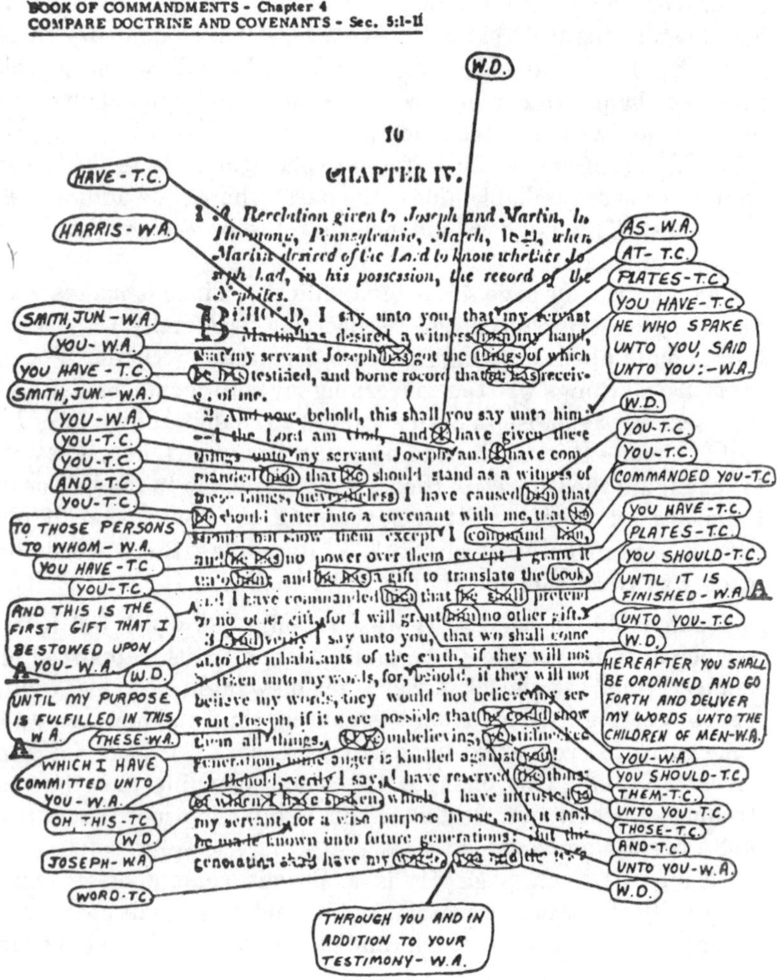

10

CHAPTER IV.

1 A Revelation given to Joseph and Martin, in
Harmony, Pennsylvania, March, 1829, when
Martin desired of the Lord to know whether Jo
seph had, in his possession, the record of the
Nephites.

BEHOLD, I say unto you, that my servant
Martin has desired a witness from my hand,
that my servant Joseph has got the things of which
he has testified, and borne record that he has received of me.
2 And now, behold, this shall you say unto him:
—I the Lord am God, and I have given these
things unto my servant Joseph, and I have commanded him that he should stand as a witness of
these things, nevertheless I have caused him that
he should enter into a covenant with me, that he
should not show them except I command him,
and he has no power over them except I grant it
unto him; and he has a gift to translate the book,
and I have commanded him that he shall pretend
to no other gift, for I will grant him no other gift.
3 And verily I say unto you, that wo shall come
unto the inhabitants of the earth, if they will not
hearken unto my words, for, behold, if they will not
believe my words, they would not believe my servant Joseph, if it were possible that he could show
them all things. O ye unbelieving, ye stiffnecked
generation, mine anger is kindled against you!
4 Behold, verily I say, I have reserved the things
of which I have spoken, which I have intrusted to
my servant, for a wise purpose in me, and it shall
be made known unto future generations: but this
generation shall have my word, [illegible] the [illegible]

BOOK OF COMMANDMENTS - Chapter 4
COMPARE DOCTRINE AND COVENANTS - Sec. 5:11-22

11

[illegible] of three of my servants shall go forth with my
words unto this generation; yea, three shall know of
a surety that these things are true, for I will give
them power, that they may behold and view these
things as they are, and to none else will I grant this
power, to receive this same testimony among this
generation. And the testimony of three witnesses
will I send forth of my word, and behold, whosoever believeth on my words, them will I visit with the
manifestation of my Spirit, and they shall be born
of me, and their testimony shall also go forth.
5 And thus, if the people of this generation harden
not their hearts, I will work a reformation among
them, and I will put down all lyings, and deceiv-
ings, and priestcrafts, and envyings, and strifes, and
idolatries, and sorceries, and all manner of iniquities, and I will establish my church, like unto the
church which was taught by my disciples in the
days of old.
6 And now if this generation do harden their
hearts against my word, behold I will deliver them
up unto satan, for he reigneth and hath much power at this time, for he hath got great hold upon the
hearts of the people of this generation: and not far
from the iniquities of Sodom and Gomorrah, do
they come at this time: and behold the sword of
justice hangeth over their heads, and if they persist in the madness of their hearts, the time cometh that it
must fall upon them. Behold I tell you these
things even as I also told the people of the destruction of Jerusalem, and my word shall be verified at
this time as it hath hitherto been verified.
7 And now I command my servant Joseph to repent, and walk more uprightly before me, and yield
to the persuasions of men no more; and that he [illegible]

43

THAT ARE GIVEN THROUGH YOU - T.C.

IN THIS THE BEGINNING OF THE RISING UP AND THE COMING FORTH OF MY CHURCH OUT OF THE WILDERNESS - CLEAR AS THE MOON, AND FAIR AS THE SUN, AND TERRIBLE AS AN ARMY WITH BANNERS. W.A.

WHOM I SHALL CALL AND ORDAIN, UNTO WHOM I WILL SHOW THESE THINGS, AND THEY - W.A.

THEY - T.C.

FROM HEAVEN WILL I DECLARE IT UNTO THEM. W.A.

OF - T.C.

WORDS - T.C.

ON - T.C.

EVEN OF WATER AND OF THE SPIRIT - AND YOU MUST WAIT YET A LITTLE WHILE, FOR YE ARE NOT YET ORDAINED - W.A.

B

W.D.

C

UNTO THE CONDEMNATION OF THIS GENERATION IF THEY HARDEN THEIR HEARTS AGAINST THEM; FOR A DESOLATING SCOURGE SHALL GO FORTH AMONG THE INHABITANTS OF THE EARTH, AND SHALL CONTINUE TO BE POURED OUT FROM TIME TO TIME, IF THEY REPENT NOT, UNTIL THE EARTH IS EMPTY, AND THE INHABITANTS THEREOF ARE CONSUMED AWAY AND UTTERLY DESTROYED BY THE BRIGHTNESS OF MY COMING. W.A.

39

YOU - W.A.

TO - W.A.

YOU - T.C.

BOOK OF COMMANDMENTS - Chapter 6
COMPARE DOCTRINE AND COVENANTS - Sec. 7:1-8

D

18

CHAPTER VI.

A Revelation given to Joseph and Oliver, in Harmony, Pennsylvania, April, 1829, when they desired to know whether John, the beloved disciple, tarried on earth. Translated from parchment, written and hid up by himself.

AND the Lord said unto me, John my beloved,
what desirest thou? and I said Lord, give
unto me power, that I may bring souls unto thee.—
And the Lord said unto me: Verily, verily I say
unto thee, because thou desiredst this, thou shalt
tarry till I come in my glory:
2 And for this cause, the Lord said unto Peter:—
If I will that he tarry till I come, what is that to
thee? for he desiredst of me that he might bring souls
unto me: but thou desiredst that thou might speed-
ily come unto me in my kingdom: I say unto thee,
Peter, this was a good desire, but my beloved has
undertaken a greater work.
3 Verily I say unto you, ye shall both have according to your desires, for ye both joy in that which
ye have desired.

FOR IF YOU SHALL ASK WHAT YOU WILL, IT SHALL BE GRANTED UNTO YOU W.A.

UNTO HIM-W.A.

LIVE AND-W.A.

OVER DEATH-W.A.

AND SHALT PROPHESY BEFORE NATIONS, KINDREDS, TONGUES AND PEOPLE-W.A.

UNTIL-T.C.

DESIRED-T.C.

MIGHTEST-T.C.

DESIRED-T.C.

THAT HE MIGHT DO MORE, OR-W.A.

YET AMONG MEN THAN WHAT HE HAS BEFORE DONE.
YEA, HE HAS UNDERTAKEN A GREATER WORK;
THEREFORE I WILL MAKE HIM AS FLAMING FIRE
AND A MINISTERING ANGEL; HE SHALL MINISTER
FOR THOSE WHO SHALL BE HEIRS OF SALVATION
WHO DWELL ON THE EARTH.
AND I WILL MAKE THEE TO MINISTER FOR
HIM AND FOR THY BROTHER JAMES; AND UNTO
YOU THREE I WILL GIVE THIS POWER AND THE
KEYS OF THIS MINISTRY UNTIL I COME. —W.A.

E

BOOK OF COMMANDMENTS - Chapter 7
COMPARE DOCTRINE AND COVENANTS - Sec. 8:1-10

19

CHAPTER VII.

1 *A Revelation given to Oliver, in Harmony, Pennsylvania, April, 1829.*

OLIVER, verily, verily I say unto you, that assuredly as the Lord liveth, which is your God and your Redeemer, even so sure shall you receive a knowledge of whatsoever things you shall ask in faith, with an honest heart, believing that you shall receive a knowledge concerning the engravings of old records, which are ancient, which contain those parts of my scripture of which have been spoken, by the manifestation of my Spirit; yea, behold I will tell you in your mind and in your heart by the Holy Ghost, which shall come upon you and which shall dwell in your heart.

2 Now, behold this is the Spirit of revelation:— behold this is the Spirit by which Moses brought the children of Israel through the Red sea on dry ground: therefore, this is thy gift; apply unto it and blessed art thou, for it shall deliver you out of the hands of your enemies, when, if it were not so, they would slay you and bring your soul to destruction.

3 O remember, these words and keep my commandments. Remember this is your gift. Now this is not all, for you have another gift, which is the gift of working with the rod: behold it has told you things: behold there is no other power save God, that can cause this rod of nature, to work in your hands, for it is the work of God; and therefore whatsoever you shall ask me to tell you by that means, that will I grant unto you, that you shall know.

4 Remember that without faith you can do noth-

COWDERY-W.A.
WHO-T.C.
SURELY-T.C.
HAS-T.C.
THY GIFT-W.A.
F ARRON-T.C.
MANY-W.A.
GIFT OF AARON TO BE WITH YOU-W.A.
THEREFORE, DOUBT NOT, -W.A.
HAVE KNOWLEDGE CONCERNING IT. T.C.
GIFT-T.C.
AND-T.C.
THE POWER OF W.A.
W.D. F
AND YOU SHALL HOLD IT IN YOUR HANDS, AND DO MARVELOUS WORKS; AND NO POWER SHALL BE ABLE TO TAKE IT AWAY OUT OF YOUR HANDS, FOR IT IS THE WORK OF GOD. -W.A.

40

19

BOOK OF COMMANDMENTS - Chapter 9
COMPARE DOCTRINE AND COVENANTS - Sec. 10:1-12

23

CHAPTER IX.

1 *A Revelation given to Joseph, in Harmony,*
Pennsylvania, May, 1829, informing him of the
alteration of the Manuscript of the fore part of
the Book of Mormon.
NOW, behold I say unto you, that because you
delivered up so many writings, which you had
power to translate, into the hands of a wicked man,
you have lost them, and you also lost your gift at the
same time, nevertheless it has been restored unto
you again: therefore, see that you are faithful and
go on unto the finishing of the remainder of the work
as you have begun. Do not run faster than you
have strength and means provided to translate, but
be diligent unto the end, that you may come off con-
queror; yea, that you may conquer satan, and those
that do uphold his work.
2 Behold they have sought to destroy you; yea,
even the man in whom you have trusted, and for
this cause I said, that he is a wicked man, for he has
sought to take away the things wherewith you have
been intrusted; and he has also sought to destroy
your gift, and because you have delivered the writings into his hands, behold they have taken them
from you: therefore, you have delivered them up;
yea, that which was sacred unto wickedness. And
behold, satan has put it into their hearts to alter the
words which you have caused to be written, or which
you have translated, which have gone out of your
hands; and behold I say unto you, that because they
have altered the words, they read contrary from that
which you translated and caused to be written; and
on this wise the devil has sought to lay a cunning

GIVEN UNTO YOU W.A.
BY THE MEANS OF THE URIM AND THUMMIM, -W.A.
AND YOUR MIND BECAME DARKENED W.A.
CONTINUE-T.C.
PRAY ALWAYS-W.A.
HAS SOUGHT TO DESTROY YOU-W.A.
HATH-T.C.
THOSE-T.C.
IS NOW-T.C.
OF TRANSLATION-W.A.
OR LABOR MORE-W.A.
ENABLE YOU TO-W.A.
THAT YOU MAY ESCAPE THE HANDS OF THE SERVANTS OF SATAN-W.A.
W.D.
WICKED MEN-T.C.

20

BOOK OF COMMANDMENTS - Chapter 15
COMPARE DOCTRINE AND COVENANTS - Sec. 18:2-11

35

Spirit in many instances, that the things which you
have written are true:
3 Wherefore you know that they are true; and if
you know that they are true, behold I give unto you
a commandment, that you rely upon the things
which are written; for in them are all things written, concerning my church, my gospel, and my
rock.

H
THE FOUNDATION OF - W.A.

H
UPON THE FOUNDATION OF W.A.

4 Wherefore if you shall build up my church, [and]
my gospel, and my rock, the gates of hell shall not
prevail against you.

W.D.

5 Behold the world is ripening in iniquity, and it
must needs be, that the children of men are stirred
up unto repentance, both the Gentiles, and also the
house of Israel:

41

HANDS-T.C.
JOSEPH SMITH, JUN. W.A.

6 Wherefore as thou hast been baptized by the
[hand] of my servant, according to that which I have
commanded him:
7 [Wherefore] he hath fulfilled the thing which I
commanded him.

W.D.

8 And now marvel not that I have called him
unto mine own purpose, which purpose is known in
me:
9 Wherefore if he shall be diligent in keeping my
commandments, he shall be blessed unto eternal
life, and his name is Joseph.

COWDERY W.A.
WHITMER W.A.

10 And now Oliver, I speak unto you, and also
unto David, by the way of commandment:
11 For behold I command all men every where
to repent, and I speak unto you, even as unto Paul
mine apostle, for you are called even with that same
calling with which he was called.
12 Remember the worth of souls is great in the
sight of God:
13 For behold the Lord your [God] suffered death

REDEEMER T.C.

B2

BOOK OF COMMANDMENTS - Chapter 24
COMPARE DOCTRINE AND COVENANTS - Sec. 20:1-12

48

2 It being regularly organized and established
agreeable to the laws of our country, by the will and
commandments of God in the fourth month and on
the sixth day of the month, which is called April:
3 Which commandments were given to Joseph,
who was called of God and ordained an apostle of
Jesus Christ, an elder of this church;
4 And also to Oliver, who was also called of God
an apostle of Jesus Christ, an elder of this church,
and ordained under his hand:
5 And this according to the grace of our Lord and
Savior Jesus Christ, to whom be all glory both now
and forever. Amen.
6 For, after that it truly was manifested unto this
first elder, that he had received a remission of his
sins, he was entangled again in the vanities of the
world;
7 But after truly repenting, God ministered unto
him by an holy angel, whose countenance was as
lightning, and whose garments were pure and white
above all whiteness, and gave unto him commandments which inspired him from on high, and gave
unto him power, by the means which were before
prepared, that he should translate a book:
8 Which book contained a record of a fallen people, and also the fulness of the gospel of Jesus
Christ to the Gentiles;
9 And also to the Jews, proving unto them, that
the holy scriptures are true;
10 And also, that God doth inspire men and call
them to his holy work, in these last days as well as
in days of old, that he might be the same God forever. Amen.
11 Which book was given by inspiration, and is
called the book of Mormon, and is confirmed to

BOOK OF COMMANDMENTS - Chapter 24
COMPARE DOCTRINE AND COVENANTS - Sec. 20:12-25

40

others by the ministering of angels, and declared
unto the world by them:
12 Wherefore having so great witnesses, by them
shall the world be judged, even as many as shall
hereafter receive this work, either to faith and righteousness, or to the hardness of heart in unbelief, to
their own condemnation, for the Lord God hath
spoken it, for we, the elders of the church, have
heard and bear witness to the words of the glorious
Majesty on high; to whom be glory forever and
ever. Amen.
13 Wherefore, by these things we know that there
is a God in heaven, who is infinite and eternal,
from everlasting to everlasting, the same unchangeable God, the maker of heaven and earth and all
things that in them is; and that he created man
male and female, and after his own image, and in
his own likeness created he them;
14 And that he gave unto the children of men
commandments, that they should love and serve
him the only being whom they should worship, but
by the transgression of these holy laws, man became
sensual and devilish, and became fallen man.
15 Wherefore, the Almighty God gave his only
begotton Son, as it is written in those scriptures,
which have been given of him, that he suffered
temptations, but gave no heed unto them;
16 That he was crucified, died, and rose again the
third day, and that he ascended into heaven to sit
down on the right hand of the Father, to reign with
Almighty power according to the will of the Father.
17 Therefore, as many as would believe and were
baptized in his holy name, and endured in faith to
the end, should be saved;

W.D.
THEREFORE-T.C.
COME TO A KNOWLEDGE OF-T.C.
SHALL RECEIVE A CROWN OF ETERNAL LIFE; W.A.
AND-T.C.
AND THOSE WHO RECEIVE IT IN T.C.
WORK-W.A.
AND REJECT IT, IT SHALL TURN-W.A.
HAS-T.C.
BUT THOSE WHO HARDEN THEIR HEARTS T.C.
W.D.
FRAMER-T.C.
WHICH ARE IN THEM; T.C.
W.D.
W.D.
THEM-T.C
LIVING AND TRUE GOD AND THAT HE SHOULD BE THE ONLY-W.A.
W.D.
W.D.
W.D.
THAT-T.C.
BE-T.C.
ENDURE-T.C.

42

21

BOOK OF COMMANDMENTS - Chapter 24
COMPARE DOCTRINE AND COVENANTS - Sec. 20:49-68

52

and take the lead of meetings; but none of these
offices is he to do when there is an elder present, but
in all cases is to assist the elder.
38 The teacher's duty is to watch over the church
always, and be with them, and strengthen them,
and see that there is no iniquity in the church, neither hardness with each other, neither lying or back-
biting, nor evil speaking;
39 And see that the church meet together often,
and also see that all the members do their duty;
40 And he is to take the lead of meetings in the
absence of the elder or priest, and is to be assisted
always, and in all his duties in the church by the
deacons;
41 But neither the teachers nor deacons have authority to baptize or administer the sacrament, but
are to warn, expound, exhort and teach, and invite
all to come unto Christ.
42 Every elder, priest, teacher or deacon, is to be
ordained according to the gifts and callings of God
unto him, by the power of the Holy Ghost which is
in the one who ordains him.
43 The several elders composing this church of
Christ, are to meet in conference once in three
months, or from time to time as they shall direct or
appoint; to do church business whatsoever is necessary.
44 And each priest or teacher, who is ordained by
a priest, is to take a certificate from him at the time,
which when presented to an elder, he is to give him
a license, which shall authorize him to perform the
duty of his calling.
45 The duty of the members after they are received by baptism.
46 The elders or priests are to have a sufficient

HE IS TO - W.A.

WHEN THERE IS NO ELDER PRESENT; BUT WHEN THERE IS AN ELDER PRESENT, HE IS ONLY TO PREACH, TEACH, EXPOUND, EXHORT, AND BAPTIZE, AND VISIT THE HOUSE OF EACH MEMBER, EXHORTING THEM TO PRAY VOCALLY AND IN SECRET AND ATTEND TO ALL FAMILY DUTIES. IN ALL THESE DUTIES THE PRIEST - T.C.

W.D.

IF OCCASION REQUIRES - W.A.

W.D.

W.D.

IF OCCASION REQUIRES W.A.

W.D.

W.D.

OR LAY ON HANDS; THEY ARE, HOWEVER, T.C.

SAID CONFERENCES T.C.

AND HE IS TO BE ORDAINED - W.A.

W.D.

AND SAID CONFERENCES ARE - W.A.

TO BE DONE AT THE TIME. THE ELDERS ARE TO RECEIVE THEIR LICENSES FROM OTHER ELDERS, BY VOTE OF THE CHURCH TO WHICH THEY BELONG, OR FROM THE CONFERENCES W.A.

WHATEVER - W.A.

W.D.

MAY - T.C.

CERTIFICATE - W.A

TO - W.A

DUTIES - T.C.

W.D

OR DEACON - W.A.

SHALL ENTITLE T.C.

I

OR HE MAY RECEIVE IT FROM A CONFERENCE. NO PERSON IS TO BE ORDAINED TO ANY OFFICE IN THIS CHURCH, WHERE THERE IS A REGULARLY ORGANIZED BRANCH OF THE SAME, WITHOUT THE VOTE OF THAT CHURCH; BUT THE PRESIDING ELDERS, TRAVELING BISHOPS, HIGH COUNCILORS, HIGH PRIESTS, AND ELDERS, MAY HAVE THE PRIVILEGE OF ORDAINING, WHERE THERE IS NO BRANCH OF THE CHURCH THAT A VOTE MAY BE CALLED. EVERY PRESIDENT OF THE HIGH PRIESTHOOD (OR PRESIDING ELDER), BISHOP, HIGH COUNCILOR, AND HIGH PRIEST, IS TO BE ORDAINED BY THE DIRECTION OF A HIGH COUNCIL OR GENERAL CONFERENCE.
W.A.

22

BOOK OF COMMANDMENTS - Chapter 26
COMPARE DOCTRINE AND COVENANTS - Sec. 25:1-11

CHAPTER XXVI.

1 *A Revelation to Emma, given in Harmony,*
Pennsylvania, July, 1830.
EMMA, my daughter in Zion, a revelation I
give unto you, concerning my will:
2 Behold thy sins are forgiven thee, and thou art
an elect lady, whom I have called.
3 Murmur not because of the things which thou
hast not seen, for they are withheld from thee, and
from the world, which is wisdom in me in a time to
come.
4 And the office of thy calling shall be for a com-
fort unto my servant Joseph, thy husband, in his
afflictions with consoling words, in the spirit of
meekness.
5 And thou shalt go with him at the time of his
going, and be unto him for a scribe, that I may send
Oliver whithersoever I will.
6 And thou shalt be ordained under his hand to
expound scriptures, and to exhort the church, according as it shall be given thee by my spirit:
7 For he shall lay his hands upon thee, and thou
shalt receive the Holy Ghost, and thy time shall be
given to writing, and to learning much.
8 And thou needest not fear, for thy husband
shall support thee in the church:
9 For unto them is his calling, that all things
might be revealed unto them, whatsoever I will according to their faith.
10 And verily I say unto thee, that thou shalt lay
aside the things of this world, and seek for the things
of a better.
11 And it shall be given thee, also, to make a se-
lection of sacred Hymns, as it shall be given thee;

HEARKEN UNTO THE VOICE OF THE LORD YOUR GOD, WHILE I SPEAK UNTO YOU, W.A.

SMITH - W.A.

AND IF THOU ART FAITHFUL AND WALK IN THE PATHS OF VIRTUE BEFORE ME, I WILL PRESERVE THY LIFE, AND THOU SHALT RECEIVE AN INHERITANCE IN ZION. W.A.

SMITH, JUN., W.A.

COWDERY W.A.

J IN - T.C.

W.D.

FOR VERILY I SAY UNTO YOU, ALL THOSE WHO RECEIVE MY GOSPEL ARE SONS AND DAUGHTERS IN MY KINGDOM. - W.A.

WHILE THERE IS NO ONE TO BE A SCRIBE FOR HIM, - W.A.

MY SERVANT W.A.

BOOK OF COMMANDMENTS - Chapter 28
COMPARE DOCTRINE AND COVENANTS - Sec. 27

K

60

CHAPTER XXVIII.

1 *A Commandment to the church of Christ, given in Harmony, Pennsylvania, September 4, 1830.*

LISTEN to the voice of Jesus Christ, your Lord, your God and your Redeemer, whose word is quick and powerful.

2 For behold I say unto you, that it mattereth
not what ye shall eat, or what ye shall drink, when
ye partake of the sacrament, if it so be that ye do
it with an eye single to my glory;

3 Remembering unto the Father my body which
was laid down for you, and my blood which was
shed for the remission of your sins:

4 Wherefore a commandment I give unto you,
that you shall not purchase wine, neither strong
drink of your enemies:

5 Wherefore you shall partake of none, except it
is made new among you, yea, in this my Father's
kingdom which shall be built up on the earth.

6 Behold this is wisdom in me, wherefore marvel
not, for the hour cometh that I will drink of the fruit
of the vine with you, on the earth, and with all those
whom my Father hath given me out of the world:

7 Wherefore lift up your hearts and rejoice, and
gird up your loins and be faithful until I come:

[illegible] Amen.

W.D.

AND TAKE UPON YOU MY WHOLE ARMOR, THAT YE MAY BE ABLE TO WITHSTAND THE EVIL DAY, HAVING DONE ALL, THAT YE MAY BE ABLE TO STAND. STAND, THEREFORE, HAVING YOUR LOINS GIRT ABOUT WITH TRUTH, HAVING ON THE BREASTPLATE OF RIGHEOUSNESS, AND YOUR FEET SHOD WITH THE PREPARATION OF THE GOSPEL OF PEACE, WHICH I HAVE SENT MINE ANGELS TO COMMIT UNTO YOU; TAKING THE SHIELD OF FAITH WHEREWITH YE SHALL BE ABLE TO QUENCH ALL THE FIERY DARTS OF THE WICKED; AND TAKE THE HELMET OF SALVATION, AND THE SWORD OF MY SPIRIT, WHICH I WILL POUR OUT UPON YOU, AND MY WORD WHICH I REVEAL UNTO YOU, AND BE AGREED AS TOUCHING ALL THINGS WHATSOEVER YE ASK OF ME, —W.A.

AND YE SHALL BE CAUGHT UP THAT WHERE I AM YE SHALL BE ALSO. —W.A.

MORONI, WHOM I HAVE SENT UNTO YOU TO REVEAL THE BOOK OF MORMON, CONTAINING THE FULNESS OF MY EVERLASTING GOSPEL, TO WHOM I HAVE COMMITTED THE KEYS OF THE RECORD OF THE STICK OF EPHRAIM; AND ALSO WITH ELIAS, TO WHOM I HAVE COMMITTED THE KEYS OF BRINGING TO PASS THE RESTORATION OF ALL THINGS SPOKEN BY THE MOUTH OF ALL THE HOLY PROPHETS SINCE THE WORLD BEGAN, CONCERNING THE LAST DAYS; AND ALSO JOHN THE SON OF ZACHARIAS, WHICH ZACHARIAS HE (ELIAS) VISITED AND GAVE PROMISE THAT HE SHOULD HAVE A SON, AND HIS NAME SHOULD BE JOHN, AND HE SHOULD BE FILLED WITH THE SPIRIT OF ELIAS; WHICH JOHN I HAVE SENT UNTO YOU, MY SERVANTS, JOSEPH SMITH, JUN., AND OLIVER COWDERY, TO ORDAIN YOU UNTO THE FIRST PRIESTHOOD WHICH YOU HAVE RECEIVED, THAT YOU MIGHT BE CALLED AND ORDAINED EVEN AS AARON; AND ALSO ELIJAH, UNTO WHOM I HAVE COMMITTED THE KEYS OF THE POWER OF TURNING THE HEARTS OF THE FATHERS TO THE CHILDREN, AND THE HEARTS OF THE CHILDREN TO THE FATHERS, THAT THE WHOLE EARTH MAY NOT BE SMITTEN WITH A CURSE; AND ALSO WITH JOSEPH AND JACOB, AND ISAAC, AND ABRAHAM, YOUR FATHERS, BY WHOM THE PROMISES REMAIN; AND ALSO WITH MICHAEL, OR ADAM, THE FATHER OF ALL, THE PRINCE OF ALL, THE ANCIENT OF DAYS; AND ALSO WITH PETER, AND JAMES, AND JOHN, WHOM I HAVE SENT UNTO YOU, BY WHOM I HAVE ORDAINED YOU AND CONFIRMED YOU TO BE APOSTLES, AND ESPECIAL WITNESSES OF MY NAME, AND BEAR THE KEYS OF YOUR MINISTRY AND OF THE SAME THINGS WHICH I REVEALED UNTO THEM; UNTO WHOM I HAVE COMMITTED THE KEYS OF MY KINGDOM, AND A DISPENSATION OF THE GOSPEL FOR THE LAST TIMES; AND FOR THE FULNESS OF TIMES, IN THE WHICH I WILL GATHER TOGETHER IN ONE ALL THINGS, BOTH WHICH ARE IN HEAVEN, AND WHICH ARE ON EARTH; AND ALSO WITH —W.A.

BOOK OF COMMANDMENTS - Chapter 44
COMPARE DOCTRINE AND COVENANTS - Sec. 42:24-36

92

committeth adultery and repenteth not, shall be
cast out; and he that committeth adultery and repenteth with all his heart, and forsaketh, and doeth
it no more, thou shalt forgive him; but if he doeth
it again, he shall not be forgiven, but shall be cast
out.
24 Thou shalt not speak evil of thy neighbor, or
do him any harm.
25 Thou knowest my laws, they are given in my
scriptures, he that sinneth and repenteth not, shall
be cast out.
26 If thou lovest me, thou shalt serve me and keep
all my commandments; and behold, thou shalt consecrate all thy properties, that which thou hast unto me, with a covenant and a deed which can not
be broken; and they shall be laid before the bishop
of my church, and two of the elders, such as he shall
appoint and set apart for that purpose.
27 And it shall come to pass, that the bishop of
my church, after that he has received the properties
of my church, that it can not be taken from the
church, he shall appoint every man a steward over
his own property, or that which he has received, inasmuch as is sufficient for himself and family:
28 And the residue shall be kept to administer to
him who has not, that every man may receive according as he stands in need:
29 And the residue shall be kept in my storehouse,
to administer to the poor and needy, as shall be appointed by the elders of the church and the bishop;
and for the purpose of purchasing lands, and the
building up of the New Jerusalem, which is hereafter to be revealed; that my covenant people may
be gathered in one, in the day that I shall come to
my temple:

BUT-T.C.
REPENTS-T.C.
W.D.
FOR THEIR SUPPORT-W.A.
L
OF-T.C.
THEM-T.C.
AND INASMUCH AS YE IMPART OF YOUR SUBSTANCE UNTO THE POOR, YE WILL DO IT UNTO ME W.A.
OR HAS APPOINTED-W.A.
AND-W.A.
AGAIN, IF THERE SHALL BE PROPERTIES IN THE HANDS OF THE CHURCH, OR ANY INDIVIDUALS OF IT, MORE THAN IS NECESSARY FOR THEIR SUPPORT AFTER THIS FIRST CONSECRATION, WHICH IS A RESIDUE TO BE CONSECRATED UNTO THE BISHOP, IT-W.A.
THOSE-T.C.
W.D.
HAVE-T.C.
THEREFORE-T.C.
AND HIS COUNCIL-W.A.
TO HIS WANTS-T.C.
HIGH COUNCIL T.C.

HAS COMMITTED T.C.
IT-W.A.
W.D.
NOR-T.C.
CONCERNING THESE THINGS-W.A.
WILT-T.C.
REMEMBER THE POOR AND-W.A.
TO IMPART-W.A.
M
OR HIGH PRIETS,-W.A.
HIS COUNSELORS, W.A.
N
AFTER THEY ARE LAID BEFORE-W.A.
THESE TESTIMONIES CONCERNING THE CONSECRATION OF-W.A.
THEY-T.C.
SHALL BE MADE ACCOUNTABLE UNTO ME-W.A.
W.D.
BY CONSECRATION-W.A.
AGREEABLE TO MY COMMANDMENTS-T.C.
BE AMPLY SUPPLIED AND-W.A.
WHO HAS NEED-W.A.
FROM TIME TO TIME-W.A.
THE-W.A.
W.D.
FOR THE PUBUC BENEFIT OF THE CHURCH AND BUILDING HOUSES OF WORSHIP-W.A.
WHEN-T.C.
THAT-T.C

23

BOOK OF COMMANDMENTS - Chapter 44
COMPARE DOCTRINE AND COVENANTS - Sec. 42:62-73

95

you in my own due time where the New Jerusalem
shall be built.
48 And behold, it shall come to pass, that my servants shall be sent both to the east, and to the west,
to the north, and to the south; and even now let
him that goeth to the east, teach them that shall be
converted to flee to the west; and this in conse-
quence of that which is to come on the earth, and
of secret combinations.
49 Behold, thou shalt observe all these things, and
great shall be thy reward.
50 Thou shalt observe to keep the mysteries of the
kingdom unto thyself, for it is not given to the world
to know the mysteries.
51 The laws which ye have received, and shall
hereafter receive, shall be sufficient for you both
here, and in the New Jerusalem.
52 Therefore, he that lacketh knowledge, let him
ask of me and I will give him liberally and upbraid
him not.
53 Lift up your hearts and rejoice, for unto you
the kingdom has been given; even so: Amen.
54 The priests and teachers, shall have their stew-
ardships given them even as the members; and the
elders are to assist the bishop in all things, and he
is to see that their families are supported out of the
property which is consecrated to the Lord, either a
stewardship, or otherwise, as may be thought best
by the elders and bishop.
55 Thou shalt contract no debts with the world,
except thou art commanded.
56 And again, the elders and bishop, shall coun-
sel together, and they shall do by the direction of
the Spirit as it must needs be necessary.
57 There shall be as many appointed as must

FORTH-T.C.
FOR UNTO YOU IT IS GIVEN TO KNOW-T.C.
YE SHALL OBSERVE W.A
CHURCH COVENANTS, SUCH AS - W.A.
OR IN OTHER WORDS, THE KEYS OF THE CHURCH - W.A.
STEWARDSHIPS-T.C.
OR HIGH PRIESTS WHO- W.A.
APPOINTED-W.A.
COUNSELORS-T.C.
OR DECIDED-W.A.
W.D.
AND THE BISHOP, ALSO, SHALL RECEIVE HIS SUPPORT, OR A JUST REMUNERATION FOR ALL HIS SERVICES IN THE CHURCH. -W.A.

COMING-T.C.
BUT UNTO THE WORLD IT IS NOT GIVEN TO KNOW THEM-T.C.
AND BE FAITHFUL-W.A.
YE-W.A.
TO-T.C.
ESTABLISH-W.A.
WISDOM-T.C.
HAVE-T.C.
W.D.
AS COUNSELERS W.A.
ARE TO HAVE-T.C.
W.D.
BISHOP,-T.C.
FOR THE GOOD OF THE POOR, AND FOR OTHER PURPOSES, AS BEFORE MENTIONED; OR THEY ARE TO RECEIVE A JUST REMUNERATION FOR ALL THEIR SERVICES, -W.A.

O

P

24

BOOK OF COMMANDMENTS - Chapter 44
COMPARE DOCTRINE AND COVENANTS - Sec. 42

95

W.D.

does be necessary to assist the bishop in obtaining places for the brethren from New-York, that they may be together as much as can be, and as they are directed by the Holy Spirit; and every family shall have a place, that they may live by themselves.—And every church shall be organized in as close bodies as they can be; and this for a wise purpose:—even so. Amen.

CHAPTER XLV. 45

A Revelation to the elders of the church, assembled in Kirtland, Ohio, given February, 1831.

O HEARKEN, ye elders of my church, and
give ear to the words which I shall speak unto you:
2 For behold, verily, verily I say unto you, that
ye have received a commandment for a law unto
my church, through him whom I have appointed
unto you, to receive commandments and revelations
from my hand.
3 And this ye shall know assuredly, that there is
none other appointed unto you to receive commandments and revelations until he be taken, if he abide
in me.
4 But verily, verily I say unto you, that none else
shall be appointed unto this gift except it be through
him, for if it be taken from him he shall not have
power, except to appoint another in his stead:
5 And this shall be a law unto you, that ye receive not the teachings of any that shall come before you as revelations or commandments:
6 And this I give unto you, that you may not be

and a deed which cannot be broken;...."[6] Later, when the doctrine proved a hard one, it was changed to: "...and consecrate of thy properties...."[7] This is a real change of doctrine. Who made the mistake, God or Joseph? This is further evidence that Joseph Smith was not from God.

A careful comparison of the photo copies will indicate the nature of the other changes.

It is interesting that in the whole Bible not one doctrine can be called in question because of a textual problem. Yet in a book about the size of our New Testament, a much later book, a book given directly to a prophet in English, there have been at least twenty doctrinal changes made. The thinking person must reject such corrupted and changed revelations. Certainly they were not from Almighty God.

The accusation that a revelation from God has been changed is a serious one. To prove that a revelation has been changed is to destroy the credibility of that work. If we could prove that the Bible had been changed by man, since it was given by God,that proof would destroy it. The Bible's accuracy has been established, while the Book of Mormon and the Doctrine and Covenants have been greatly changed, revised, and edited. Other serious accusations can be made against the Doctrine and Covenants. Observe the following as examples of the types of problems found.

The Word of Wisdom

The document normally referred to by the Latter-day Saints as "The Word of Wisdom," is the 89th section of the Doctrine and Covenants. It is this document which teaches against the drinking of coffee or tea. It is a rather ridiculous little document. The Mormon Church does not go by all of its teachings, only parts of it. Actually it does not condemn coffee or tea, but hot drinks, yet little is said against hot chocolate by the church. In times past cola drinks were condemned, but this teaching has now been reversed, possibly because U & I Sugar, a Mormon-owned company, sells large quantities of sugar to the Coca-Cola Company.

In verse five of this 89th section we are told what elements are

[6] Book of Commandments 28:26.

[7] Doctrine and Covenants 42:30.

to be used to observe the sacraments (Lord's Supper).

> That inasmuch as any man drinketh wine or strong drink among you, behold it is not good, neither meet in the spirit of your Father, only in assembling yourselves together to offer up your sacraments before him. And behold this should be wine, yea, pure wine of the grape of the vine, of your own make.[8]

In spite of the fact that the instruction seems quite plain, the Mormon Church uses water in the communion cup. Why observe one part that teaches against hot drinks and not observe the other that teaches how communion is to be observed?

A further examination discloses some advice about how to treat sick cattle. "And again, tobacco is not for the body, neither for the belly, and it not good for man, but is an herb for bruises and all sick cattle, to be used with judgment and skill."[9] The word in question here is the word "all." Is tobacco for "all sick cattle?" It would seem very unlikely.

Further along in this same section we have advice about the use of meat. It is hard to tell whether we are to be vegetarians or meat eaters.

> Yea, flesh also of beasts and of the fowls of the air, I, the Lord, have ordained for the use of man with thanksgiving; nevertheless they are to be used sparingly; And it is pleasing unto me that they should not be used, only in times of winter, or of cold or famine.... And these hath God made for the use of man only in times of famine and excess of hunger.[10]

Does the Mormon church believe and teach this? Certainly not. Meat is a regular thing in their diet during every season. Why live by one part and neglect the others? It is difficult to understand a church that will enforce one verse and reject the next.

Many Gods

The Book of Mormon is purely monotheistic. It is the Doctrine and Covenants that introduces the doctrine of polytheism. In section 121 we read: "At time to come in the which nothing shall be withheld, whether there be one God or many gods, they shall be manifest."[11] Later in the same section we see a further hint of the

---

8 *Ibid.*, 89:5-6.

9 *Ibid.*, 89:8.

10 *Ibid.*, 89:12-15.

11 *Ibid.*, 121:28.

introduction of this new doctrine.

> According to that which was ordained in the midst of the Council of the Eternal God of all other gods before this world was, that should be reserved unto the finishing and the end thereof, when every man shall enter into his eternal presence and into his immortal rest.[12]

This is the beginning of the doctrine of eternal progression, which teaches that men can learn to be gods. A much more complete discussion of this subject will be made in Part III.

Polygamy

The Book of Mormon takes a strong stand against polygamy. It is the Doctrine and Covenants that introduces the subject. Section 132 deals extensively with this matter. Notice the following quotation.

> Verily, thus saith the Lord unto you my servant Joseph, that inasmuch as you have inquired of my hand to know and understand wherein I, the Lord, justified my servants Abraham, Isaac, and Jacob, as also Moses, David and Solomon, my servants, as touching the principle and doctrine of their having many wives and concubines...Therefore, prepare thy heart to receive and obey the instructions which I am about to give unto you; for all those who have this law revealed unto them must obey the same. For behold, I reveal unto you a new and an everlasting covenant; and if ye abide not that covenant, then are ye damned; for no one can reject this covenant and be permitted to enter into my glory.[13]

So polygamy is introduced as a new and everlasting covenant that must be obeyed by all who have it revealed to them. If they refuse to obey it they are to be damned.

Later in the same section we read:

> David also received many wives and concubines, and also Solomon and Moses my servants, as also many others of my servants, from the beginning of creation until this time; and in nothing did they sin save in those things which they received not of me. David's wives and concubines were given unto him of me, by the hand of Nathan, my servant, and others of the prophets who had the keys of this power; and in none of these things did he sin against me save in the case of Uriah and his wife;...I am the Lord thy God, and I gave unto thee, my servant Joseph, an appointment and restore all things. Ask what ye will, and it shall be given unto you according to my word.[14]

---

12 *Ibid.*, 121:32.

13 *Ibid.*, 132:1,3-4.

14 *Ibid.*, 132:38-40.

Even though this section is wordy and it appears that Joseph Smith is trying to appease his wife about this matter, yet the thread is clear. Joseph is instituting polygamy. It was understood this way by the Latter-day Saints, and was practiced until the United States forced them to quit years later. For the church today to deny this fact is dishonest. What this section says is clear, and what was practiced by Joseph Smith and Brigham Young and a long succession of Mormons is a matter of recorded history.

In the same section Joseph's purpose can be further seen.

> And again, as pertaining to the law of the priesthood—if any man espouse a virgin, and desire to espouse another, and the first give her consent, and if he espouse the second, and they are virgins, and have vowed to no other man, then is he justified; he cannot commit adultery for they are given unto him; for he cannot commit adultery with that that belongeth unto him and to no one else. And if he have ten virgins given unto him by this law, he cannot commit adultery, for they belong to him, and they are given unto him; therefore is he justified.[15]

No doubt is left as to what Joseph Smith was about in this section. It is the institution of polygamy. Is this God's plan for man? Was God ever really pleased by polygamy?

When God made Adam he only made one wife for him. He taught, "Therefore shall a man leave his father and his mother, and shall cleave unto his wife...."[16] You notice it says "wife," not "wives." It is true that Abraham, Moses, David, Solomon, and many others had many wives. Yet did God command it, or did he simply permit it? Every case of polygamy in the Bible caused problems for those involved in it. Abraham became the father of two nations and they have fought ever since. Solomon's wives turned his heart away from God. Therefore, it is no surprise that in the New Testament instruction is given that the leaders of the church are to have only one wife.

> A bishop then must be blameless, the husband of one wife, vigilant, sober, of good behavior, given to hospitality, apt to teach;...Let the deacons be the husband of one wife, ruling their children and their own houses well.[17]
>
> For this cause left I thee in Crete, that thou shouldest set in order the things that are wanting, and ordain elders in every city, as I had appointed thee: If

---

15 *Ibid.*, 132:61-62.

16 Genesis 2:24.

17 I Timothy 3:2, 12.

any be blameless, the husband of one wife, having faithful children not accused of riot or unruly.[18]

So polygamy is condemned in the New Testament and also in the Book of Mormon (Jacob 2:24-27), and then endorsed and commanded in the Doctrine and Covenants. Is God that confused about the matter? It is difficult to accept such contradictory "revelations" as having their origin with God.

Chapter VI

A PEARL OF GREAT PRICE

The Pearl of Great Price is a small volume made up of three parts; the books of Moses, Abraham, and Joseph Smith. It is this volume that presents the most damaging evidence against Joseph Smith. In this volume we have proof positive that Joseph Smith was not capable of translating any foreign document.

The book of Abraham begins with a few comments in the heading above the text which says, "A Translation of some ancient Records, that have fallen into our hands from the catacombs of Egypt.—The writings of Abraham while he was in Egypt, called the Book of Abraham, written by his own hand, upon papyrus."[1]

This would be fantastic information, if it were true. Can you imagine having the very own handwriting of Father Abraham? It would be the only instance of an original handwritten document of any Bible writer. We are immediately skeptical, since Abraham lived so long ago and we do not have any other Bible author's original manuscript.

Several things make one skeptical about it being possible for such a document to exist. First, papyrus is durable, but not durable enough that it could last for nearly four thousand years in an alligator skin, which is where the archaeologists who sold the manuscript to Joseph Smith are said to have found it. Yet this is the claim that Joseph made for the document.

---

[18] Titus 1:5-6.

[1] Pearl of Great Price, preface to The Book of Abraham.

When Joseph Smith translated the document into the Book of Abraham he made a hand written copy. He placed the Egyptian character in the left hand column and then explained what it meant on the right side of the paper. For years this hand written copy has been available by photo reprint, but the original Egyptian papyrus was lost. It was supposedly destroyed by the great Chicago fire of 1871.

In 1967 the papyrus was found and presented to the Latter-day Saint Church by The Metropolitan Museum of Art of New York. Thinking that Joseph Smith couldn't possibly have made a mistake, or lied, the church allowed it to be photographed and published in *Dialogue Magazine.* The cat was out of the bag, for this photo copy was submitted to three different Egyptologists for them to independently translate. Each translated it into about seventy words, each with almost identical meanings, each agreeing that it was a quite common type of document that had to do with funerals in Egypt.

Joseph Smith came nowhere close to the meaning that it really had, when he wrote his book of Abraham. In fact, Joseph Smith made it into over four thousand words. This means some characters had to be translated into seventy-five to one hundred or more words, and this from just one Egyptian letter.[2]

We must conclude that Joseph Smith couldn't translate a foreign document. After many years we now have proof that Joseph Smith was a fraud. We do not have the gold plates, but if there were gold plates, and Joseph Smith did seek to translate them, you can be sure he made a mess of it.

It is the Book of Abraham that was the basis of the doctrine that a Negro could not hold the priesthood in the Mormon Church. A white boy of twelve could hold the priesthood, but a Negro could not.[3] In the book of Abraham we read:

> Now, Pharaoh being of that lineage by which he could not have the right of Priesthood, not withstanding the Pharaohs would fain claim it from Noah through Ham, therfore my father was led away by their idolatry.[4]

---

2 For a complete treatment of this subject, I would recommend for reading, Chapter 22 of *Mormonism—Shadow or Reality?* by Jerald Tanner and Sandra Tanner, enl. ed. (Salt Lake City, Utah: Modern Microfilm Co., 1972).

3 A more complete study of this subject is given in Part III, Chapter IX. This doctrine was changed June 9, 1978.

4 Pearl of Great Price, Abraham 1:27.

The Bible teaches that all people are equal in Christ regardless of the color of their skin or race.

> There is neither Jew nor Greek, there is neither bond nor free, there is neither male nor female: for ye are all one in Christ Jesus. And if ye be Christ's, then are ye Abraham's seed, and heirs according to the promise.[5]

Chapter VII

A SUMMARY

What does a comparison of the Bible, Book of Mormon, Doctrine and Covenants, and Pearl of Great Price show? It demonstrates that the Bible is remarkably accurate. Although the Bible is an ancient book and the others are modern books, we find that the Bible has been preserved with such integrity that not one significant doctrine can be called in question. Yes, there are a few textual problems, due to its age and the thousands of copies we have of it in Hebrew and Greek. Yet the problems are not problems of revision and changing it. The textual problems are the kind one would expect from such an ancient book.

It is remarkable that such old manuscript finds as the Dead Sea Scrolls, the Bodmer II Text of the Gospel of John, the Vatican, Sinatic, and Alexandrean Manuscripts, all give us undeniable proof that our Bible is accurate.

After a close examination of a much later book, The Book of Mormon, we find that it was filled with mistakes, errors of chronology, grammar, and indications of the ignorance of the one who originally wrote it. Yet it claims to have been translated into English by the power of God. Is it reasonable to blame God for these mistakes?

How can we hope to explain all the indications that the Book of Mormon was written at a much later date than it claims? How can it claim to have been written from 600 B.C. to A.D. 421 and yet quote from the King James translation of the Bible so often? How do we explain the reference to modern scientific discoveries? Why is it filled with theological problems?

The Book of Mormon has failed every test: the test of accuracy,

---

[5] Galatians 3:28-29.

the test of antiquity, the test of honesty. In every way it has been proved that it cannot be scripture from God, except the one-third that is a direct quotation from the King James Bible.

A close examination of the Doctrine and Covenants showed many serious problems. While it makes a definite claim to being a direct revelation from God, never to pass away or be changed, we found that there were 2,786 changes, including more than twenty doctrinal changes. How could a thinking person accept it as scripture? Probably it is the most changed book ever to have claimed to be scripture.

There is such a vast difference between the integrity of the Bible and that of the Doctrine and Covenants that one is forced to conclude that it is not the work of God.

Such ridiculous sections as the one on polygamy and the Word of Wisdom clearly show us that it is not a revelation from God.

The Pearl of Great Price supplies the most damaging evidence against Joseph Smith. His claim to have translated the Book of Abraham from some Egyptian papyrus has been completely proven false. One Egyptian scholar said if he had to grade his paper he would be forced to give him a zero, because he hadn't gotten even one thing right.

It is clear that the Bible is a book from God, divine in its origin, carefully preserved for us today. Every test has been passed by the Bible. The critics have tried to destroy it but have not had grounds to do so. The Bible has stood.

Yet Mormon scripture, The Book of Mormon, Doctrine and Covenants, and Pearl of Great Price have not stood the test. Investigation has destroyed them. People who know the truth about them should not still cling to them. In the light of modern research and evidence it is likely that enlightened people will more and more turn from them. When the system does fall it is likely that their scriptures will be a major factor in this fall.

Part II

TRUE AND FALSE PROPHETS

Chapter VIII

THE BIBLE AND PROPHETS

"For there shall arise false Christs, and false prophets, and shall shew great signs and wonders; insomuch that, if it were possible, they shall deceive the very elect."[1]

The claim that is made for Joseph Smith is that he is a prophet from God. It is an easy matter to make a claim; it is a little harder to substantiate that claim by the scriptures. Does Joseph Smith bear the marks or signs of a true prophet of God? Does he measure up to the teachings of the Bible as to what a prophet should be? Does the Bible teach that there are to be prophets today? These questions need to be answered.

If you were to take a tour of the beautiful, new Visitors Information Center at Temple Square in Salt Lake City, Utah, as a part of that tour you would be told about all the great prophets of old. Such men as Enoch, Noah, Abraham, Moses, and Isaiah would likely be mentioned. This would be done in the setting of the most lavish surroundings of fine architecture and beautiful paintings. You would be led by an articulate, well-educated, and well-dressed guide. He would point out that in times past God raised up John the Baptist, then Paul, and each because of the great need. Later in history when there was a great need, men like Martin Luther, John Wesley, and Calvin were raised up. After one has gotten in the habit of saying "Yes," it is affirmed that in just such a way God raised up Joseph Smith, Jr., to bring the people back to God. In the surroundings of the expensive visitors information center and with a polished guide who can make Mormonism sound so wonderful, many people are baptized into the

---

1 Matthew 24:24.

Mormon Church before they continue their journey from Salt Lake City. One must give them credit for doing a superb job of selling their religion. Yet, what does the Bible really say about this matter?

Eight Bible Passages on Prophets

The question might be asked, "Do signs and wonders prove that a prophet is of God?" We would answer, "No." Even if a person can work notable signs and wonders, yet if he instructs us to go contrary to the instructions we have from Jehovah God already, we are not to follow that prophet.

> If there arise among you a prophet, or a dreamer of dreams, and giveth thee a sign or a wonder, and the sign or the wonder come to pass, whereof he spake unto thee, saying, Let us go after other gods, which thou hast not known, and let us serve them; Thou shalt not hearken unto the words of that prophet, or that dreamer of dreams: for the Lord your God proveth you, to know whether ye love the Lord your God with all your heart and with all your soul. Ye shall walk after the Lord your God, and fear him, and keep his commandments and obey his voice, and ye shall serve him, and cleave unto him. And that prophet, or that dreamer of dreams, shall be put to death; because he hath spoken to turn you away from the Lord your God, which brought you out of the land of Egypt, and redeemed you out of the house of bondage, to thrust thee out of the way which the Lord thy God commanded thee to walk in. So shalt thou put the evil away from the midst of thee.[2]

The instruction is quite clear. Miracles, signs, or dreams are not enough to prove that one is a prophet. If the prophet does not teach and keep the commandments of God that have already been given, then he is to be rejected. Even if this prophet can predict the future he is not to be received.

Today, people have often been led to false teaching by someone who seems to be able to work some sign or wonder. If a supposed prophet can predict the future with some sort of accuracy, or "speak in tongues," then people are inclined to listen to whatever he has to say as the gospel truth.

In establishing a rule to deal with supposed prophets, we should first ask, "Does he follow the proven commands of God?" If he does not, then we cannot accept him as a prophet.

A second passage of scripture that is even more forceful comes

---

[2] Deuteronomy 13:1-5.

from the book of Zechariah. In order to understand this scripture one needs to be familiar with what goes before and after it. In the twelfth chapter we have what are recognized as definite predictions about Jesus Christ.

> And I will pour upon the house of David, and upon the inhabitants of Jerusalem, the spirit of Grace and of supplications: and they shall look upon me whom they have pierced, and they shall mourn for him, as one mourneth for his only son, and shall be in bitterness for him, as one that is in bitterness for his firstborn.[3]

In the light of the context of the twelfth and thirteenth chapters, it is clear that this is talking about Jesus. The one who would be pierced was to be of the house of David. The event would take place in Jerusalem. They did not pierce Zechariah. The mourning was for an only son. Without a doubt it is a prediction about Jesus Christ and his death, since He himself applied this context to himself.[4]

In the thirteenth chapter we have another prediction about Jesus. "Awake, O Sword, against my shepherd, and against the man that is my fellow, saith the Lord of hosts: smite the shepherd, and the sheep shall be scattered: and I will turn mine hand upon the little ones."[5] Christ himself indicated that this passage was talking about his being taken away from among the apostles. There can be no doubt that Jesus Himself considered this a Messianic prophecy.

Right in the midst of such clear predictions we have another clear prophecy about Jesus Christ.

> In that day there shall be a fountain opened to the house of David and to the inhabitants of Jerusalem for sin and uncleanness. And it shall come to pass in that day, saith the Lord of hosts, that I will cut off the names of the idols out of the land, and they shall no more be remembered: and also I will cause the prophets and the unclean spirit to pass out of the land. And it shall come to pass, that when any shall yet prophesy, then his father and his mother that begat him shall say unto him, Thou shalt not live; for thou speakest lies in the name of the Lord: and his father and his mother that begat him shall thrust him through when he prophesieth.[6]

---

[3] Zechariah 12:10.

[4] Matthew 26:31.

[5] Zechariah 13:7.

[6] *Ibid.*, 13:1-3.

This isn't one of the easiest passages of scripture to understand. A further explanation might be helpful. A fountain or spring in Israel was a great blessing. For the most part the land is dry. Wells and springs have always been at a premium. So he speaks of Christ's coming as a fountain. It is a spiritual fountain. This fountain was to be of the house of David; we know that Jesus came of the house and lineage of David. This would happen in Jerusalem; Jesus was crucified just about 150 or possible 200 yards beyond the walls of Jerusalem. This fountain was to be for sin and uncleanness; Christ came to save His people from their sins; He washed our sins away. The obvious conclusion is that this passage is talking about the day of Christ's life and sacrifice.

It says, "in that day...I will cause the prophets...to pass out of the land."[7] The question needs to be answered as to whether this was a twenty-four hour day or a longer period of time. It is clear from observing the period under discussion that the prophet Zechariah did not mean a literal twenty-four hour day but a period of time, probably the lifetime of Jesus.

So with Christ's generation passing, we would expect that there should be no more prophets. A careful look at church history will show that when those that received the special gifts of the Holy Spirit passed off the scene, there were no more prophets, except false ones.

In the words of Zechariah, "if any shall yet prophesy, they speak lies in the name of Jehovah."[8] So when those last ones, given special gifts by the apostles passed off the scene, we would expect that there would be no more prophets.

Let's not rest our case entirely on this passage, but see what other scriptures have to say about this matter. Jesus had quite a bit to say about the matter of prophets. In the Sermon on the Mount He warned about false prophets coming and leading many astray.

> Beware of false prophets, which come to you in sheep's clothing, but inwardly they are ravening wolves. Ye shall know them by their fruits.... Not every one that saith unto me, Lord, Lord, shall enter into the kingdom of heaven; but he that doeth the will of my Father which is in heaven. Many

---

[7] *Ibid.*

[8] *Ibid.*

will say to me in that day, Lord, Lord, have we not prophesied in thy name? and in thy name have cast out devils? and in thy name done many wonderful works? And then will I profess unto them, I never knew you: depart from me, ye that work iniquity. Therefore whosoever heareth these sayings of mine, and doeth them, I will liken him unto a wise man, which built his house upon a rock; and the rain descended, and the floods came, and the winds blew, and beat upon that house; and it fell not: for it was founded upon a rock. And every one that heareth these sayings of mine, and doeth them not, shall be likened unto a foolish man, which built his house upon the sand: And the rain descended, and the floods came, and the winds blew, and beat upon that house; and it fell: and great was the fall of it.[9]

Jesus warns us that just because a person says that he is a prophet is not enough proof. We must observe his fruits. Of course the Mormon people point to the fruits of Joseph Smith's teachings and say that it is good. Yet, it is not enough that one has a few good works. One must do the will of the Father in heaven. Those who built on the sand heard the words of Jesus and did not do them. There are many instances where Joseph Smith directly violated the very clear teachings of Jesus.[10]

At this point, though, we only want to stress that Jesus warned that there would be false prophets. Jesus told us how we could determine who was a false prophet and who was not. Those who hear his words and do not do them definitely are false prophets. When one claims to have good fruit and yet does not obey the teachings of Jesus, his claim is false. Disobedience to Jesus is an open indication that one is not a prophet of God.

Jesus again warns of false prophets by saying, "For there shall arise false Christs, and false prophets, and shall shew great signs and wonders; insomuch that, if it were possible, they shall deceive the very elect."[11]

We ask the question, "Who have the false prophets been?" Jesus said they would come. Jesus certainly would not make an idle threat. Jesus warned that they would shew great signs and wonders and deceive many people. We are not surprised when we see divergent movements, led by prophets, each claiming to be from God, yet teaching contrary and conflicting doctrines. Jesus said it would be so. We certainly need to ask ourselves, "Is it

---

9 Matthew 7:15-27.

10 Part III of this book deals with thirteen such instances of departures from the teachings of Jesus.

11 Matthew 24:24.

possible that Jesus had Joseph Smith in mind?" We will want to examine the Bible's teaching to be sure that Joseph Smith has not led us away from the teachings of Jesus Christ and His apostles.

The Apostle Paul often warned about the danger of false prophets. Paul realized that the devil was powerful and actively at work seeking to lead the people away from God. If it took religion to lead the people astray, then he would raise up false prophets.

We are not surprised, therefore when Paul says:

> I marvel that ye are so soon removed from him that called you into the grace of Christ unto another gospel: Which is not another; but there be some that trouble you, and would pervert the gospel of Christ. But though we, or an angel from heaven, preach any other gospel unto you than that which we have preached unto you, let him be accursed. As we said before, so say I now again, If any man preach any other gospel unto you than that which we have preached unto you, let him be accursed.[12]

Paul minces no words. The test of a preacher or prophet is, Does he preach the same message? If he comes with a different gospel, even if he is an angel, he is to be rejected. The test that we will want to apply to Joseph Smith is, Does he proclaim the same gospel message? Does he teach the same doctrine about God, Christ, the Holy Spirit, the Lord's Supper, the Virgin Birth, revelation, and such matters? If he does not, we cannot accept him.

The burden of proof rests upon those who claim to have a modern-day prophet to show that he teaches the same things Jesus and the Apostles did. If it can be demonstrated that it is a different gospel, then it must be rejected.

Many Christians today believe that we are in the last days. We know that we live in the last dispensation of time and probably in the last days of that dispensation. We are warned by the Holy Spirit to be extra careful in these days. "Now the Spirit speaketh expressly, that in the latter times some shall depart from the faith, giving heed to seducing spirits, and doctrines of devils; Speaking lies in hypocrisy; having their conscience seared with a hot iron."[13]

---

12 Galatians 1:6-9.

13 I Timothy 4:1-2.

Since we are warned that many of these false teachers will come, then we should give special care not to be taken in by them. Every effort must be expended to examine the teachings of the Bible thoroughly and compare them carefully with anyone claiming that he is a prophet of God.

The Apostle John gives good advice about how to know who is of God and who is not of God. Often when we begin to question the claims of another religion, someone will say, "Judge not that ye be not judged," or "I don't talk about politics or religion." Because of such poor reasoning we have error running rampant through our world. Would we use the same reasoning about dirty food, or drugs? In fact, we have an inspired Apostle telling us to examine closely one who claims to be a prophet.

> Beloved, believe not every spirit, but try the spirits whether they are of God: because many false prophets are gone out into the world. Hereby know ye the Spirit of God: Every spirit that confesseth that Jesus Christ is come in the flesh is of God: And every spirit that confesseth not that Jesus Christ is come in the flesh is not of God: and this is that spirit of anti-christ, whereof ye have heard that it should come; and even now already is it in the world. Ye are of God, little children, and have overcome them: because greater is he that is in you, than he that is in the world. They are of the world, and the world heareth them. We are of God: he that knoweth God heareth us; he that is not of God heareth not us. Hereby know we the spirit of truth, and the spirit of error.[14]

We have the command of the beloved Apostle John to examine those who claim to be prophets. It is not an unchristian attitude that makes one do this, but a following of apostolic instruction. Truth is not hurt by examination, it is helped.

The Apostle explains that we must submit our lives to their teachings if we are to prove we are of God. John affirms that "we are of God."[15] This is speaking about "we Apostles." He says that if we hear them, then we are of God. If we do not hear them we are not of God. We can tell the spirit of truth and the spirit of error by whether we hear them or not.

We want to examine the teachings of the Latter-day Saints Church by the teachings of the Apostles. If they measure up, fine; if they do not we cannot accept them.

---

14 I John 4:1-6.

15 *Ibid.*

One last scripture comes from the very last few verses of the Bible. Most Latter-day Saints have been taught that this verse of scripture only applies to the book of Revelation. If any holds this view, he should think about these questions. If it is wrong to add to the book of Revelations would it be any better to do so with Romans? If it is wrong to take away from the book of Revelation would it be any better to do so with Matthew? Of course not. Therefore the truth expressed must apply to the whole Bible.

> For I testify unto every man that heareth the words of the prophecy of this book, If any man shall add unto these things, God shall add unto him the plagues that are written in this book: And if any man shall take away from the words of the book of this prophecy, God shall take away his part out of the book of life, and out of the holy city, and from the things which are written in this book.[16]

What a solemn warning. It stands as a sentinel at the very close of the scriptures, reminding us that we are to hear and obey its words. We are to be careful to protect and uphold its teachings to observe and preserve them.

Moses came as a lawgiver from God. Exodus and Deuteronomy give the laws that were given by God through him. In the future generations, until the time of Christ, all the prophets turned people back to Moses. Not one new doctrine was ever added to the teachings of Moses. Why? Because the laws and commands were from God. It only stands to reason that such laws should be observed. So the later prophets did not introduce new teachings. Some of what they said was new, since they were predictions of the future, but not even one change of doctrine came through the later prophets.

So it was with Jesus Christ. He came as the Divine lawgiver. He set up His church and instituted its laws and rules that were for all time. If anyone claims to be a prophet from God, he must only point people back to the lawgiver, Jesus. When one does any more or less than that he has proven beyond a shadow of a doubt to be a false prophet.

Since the Bible teaches that after Jesus' day there would be no more prophets, except false prophets, we cannot accept Joseph Smith as a true prophet of God. Since the Bible warns us over and

---

[16] Revelation 22:18-19.

over again not to accept anyone who teaches a different doctrine, we must reject Joseph Smith, since he introduced many new doctrines, changed existing doctrine, and contradicted the clear teachings of Jesus and His apostles.[17]

Part III

THIRTEEN FALSE DOCTRINES

Chapter IX

THE BIBLE AND MORMON TEACHING COMPARED

"But the hour cometh, and now is, when the true worshippers shall worship the Father in spirit and in truth: for the Father seeketh such to worship him."[1]

Often today people wonder why religious people are so concerned about the teachings of the church. In our permissive society, where almost anything goes, the attitude is, why be concerned about what the church teaches? Should not Christians just love one another and do as they please? What difference does it make what we believe or teach? It makes a lot of difference.

Why are we concerned? First, pure doctrine is as important as pure food, water, or drugs. When we do not have pure food we have sick people. When we do not have pure doctrine we have hurt people. People can become emotionally and spiritually sick because of false doctrine. It is always true that error hurts people. When we have false teaching or ignorance, it will ultimately hurt these people that hold it as truth. Beyond this, we should want to know what is right, just because it is right. Jesus said, "And ye shall know the truth, and the truth shall make you free."[2]

One Mormon leader excused the many theological and doc-

---

[17] Part III of this study will discuss some of the many doctrinal changes that Joseph Smith made.

[1] John 4:23.

[2] *Ibid.*, 8:32.

trinal problems in the Mormon Church by saying that every church has its doctrinal problems and he wasn't surprised that they did, too. That is a real "cop out," to use a modern expression. Can we just shrug our shoulders and say everyone else has problems so I might as well have some too? It would be as reasonble to say that since one-third of the earth is hungry, I won't feed my children either. Or, many people are dirty so I'll not take a bath either. The rest of the world has inflation, so America might as well have it, too. This is the very attitude that brings decay in governments and churches. Let us therefore observe thirteen important doctrinal departures from the Bible that are practiced by the Mormon Church.

The Doctrine of God

If we have a false doctrine about God we are in trouble from the beginning. Just as a house that does not have a good foundation cannot be sound no matter how many stories one might add above, so a religion that has a false doctrine about God can never be sound.

What is the Morman doctrine of God? It can be summed up in a little poem of unknown origin.

> As man now is, God once was;
> As God now is, man may be.
> A son of God, like God to be
> Would not be robbing deity.[3]

To the average Christian, and even to some Mormon folk, this statement sounds repugnant, yet it is an actual statement of Latter-day Saint doctrine. It is often quoted by Mormon church leaders and is their current doctrinal position. This statement is normally phrased: "As man now is, God once was; as God now is man may become." This is a part of the doctrine of eternal progression, which is, briefly stated, that man has lived before, is now what he is because of what he did in his previous existence,

---

[3] After hearing the above poem quoted many times, and in an effort to substantiate it, I called the church offices and asked concerning its source. I was told that Lorenzo Snow, Prophet and Revelator of the Latter-day Saint Church, had first put this doctrine in print in 1919, in the June issue of the *Improvement Era*. I was told that this same doctrine was stated by Brigham Young at Joseph Smith, Jr.'s funeral. It is generally conceded that these "truths" are in the Doctrine and Covenants, Section 121, verses 28 and 32. During this telephone conversation with the authorities at the L.D.S. Church office building, they readily agreed that this is a fair statement of their position and often quoted poem.

and will become in the next life what he has prepared himself to become by his preparation in this life. Man progresses until he reaches "Godhood." God Himself once was a man, now is God; man will also have this opportunity. This doctrine is a doctrine of many gods. In short, Mormons are not monotheistic, but polytheistic. They believe in many galaxies over which elevated men now rule. This doctrine conceives of God as having body, parts, and passions.

Brigham Young, a Mormon prophet, revelator, and seer, said of Adam: "He is our Father and our God, and the only God with whom we have to do."[4] Another oft-quoted statement, attributed to Joseph Smith, is:

> God himself was once as we are now, and is an exalted man...if you were to see him today, you would see him like yourselves, in all the person, image and very form of man, and you have got to learn how to be Gods yourselves...the same as all Gods have done before you.[5]

And again:

> First, God himself, who sits enthroned in yonder heavens, is a man like unto one of yourselves, that is the great secret...God himself; the Father of us all dwelt on an earth the same as Jesus Christ himself did,...You have got to learn how to be gods yourselves...No man can learn you more than what I have told you.[6]

Is this a true Christian doctrine? Is it taught in the scriptures? Did Christ teach this doctrine? I would cite a few verses of scripture and the matter should be clear. "Ye are my witnesses, saith the Lord, and my servant whom I have chosen: that ye may know and believe me, and understand that I am he: before me there was no God formed, neither shall there be after me."[7]

This statement is in direct contradiction to Mormon teaching. There is a direct contradiction between the Biblical Isaiah, and Mormonism's Lorenzo Snow, Joseph Smith, and Brigham Young. This is only the beginning of what Isaiah has to say. Notice: "Is

---

[4] G. D. Watt, ed., *Journal of Discourses*, by Brigham Young, 26 vols., (Liverpool: F.D. & S.W. Richards, 1854; reprint ed., Salt Lake City, Utah, 1966), 1:50.

[5] Franklin D. Richards and James A. Little, ed., *A Compendium of The Doctrine of the Gospel*, 2nd. ed. (Salt Lake City, Utah: Deseret News Company, 1884), p. 238.

[6] Joseph Smith, *Times and Seasons*, vol. 5, pp. 613-614, cited by Jerald Tanner and Sandra Tanner, *Mormonism—Shadow or Reality?* (Salt Lake City, Utah: Modern Microfilm, 1964), p. 137.

[7] Isaiah 43:10.

there a God beside me? yea, there is no God: I know not any."[8] If God didn't know of any other god, our trio of prophets certainly did not know of any.

Isaiah makes the matter more clear:

> I am the Lord, and there is none else, there is no God beside me: I girded thee, though thou hast not known me: That they may know from the rising of the sun, and from the west, that there is none beside me. I am the Lord, and there is none else.[9]

Apparently God wanted men to know this fact clearly, for it is repeated over and over again.

Probably the clearest of the passages in Isaiah is this one:

> Remember the former things of old: for I am God, and there is none else; I am God, and there is none like me, Declaring the end from the beginning, and from ancient times the things that are not yet done, saying, My counsel shall stand, and I will do all my pleasure.[10]

If, in truth, God does know the end from the beginning, then he would know for sure if there were any other gods.

Jesus only knew there to be one God. "And Jesus said unto him, Why callest thou me good? there is none good but one, that is, God."[11] "And this is life eternal, that they might know thee the only true God, and Jesus Christ, whom thou hast sent."[12]

Paul the Apostle said, "As concerning therefore the eating of those things that are offered in sacrifice unto idols, we know that an idol is nothing in the world, and that there is none other God but one."[13]

Mormon teaching says man can become God, and God once was a man. The Bible says there is but one God. There is none else, never has been, and never will be. If you can be polytheistic (believing in many gods), then you can be a Mormon. If you accept the doctrine that as man now is, God once was, and as God now is, man may become, you do not believe in the God of the Bible.

No more serious accusation could be made against a religious movement than that it did not believe in one supreme being, one

---

8 *Ibid.*, 44:8.

9 *Ibid.*, 45:5-6.

10 *Ibid.*, 46:9-10.

11 Mark 10:18.

12 John 17:3.

13 I Corinthians 8:4.

who rules everything throughout all the universe. This is the whole basis of Christianity. Almost all other religious bodies, claiming to be Christian, throughout the world, believe in one supreme being. The Mormons are the exception. This is one good, clear reason why it is not reasonable to accept the claims of the Mormon system.

The Doctrine About Jesus Christ

According to universal Christian teaching, it is absolutely necessary that we know Jesus Christ, if we are to be saved. "Neither is there salvation in any other: for there is none other name under heaven given among men, whereby we must be saved."[14]

If a movement tries to dishonor Jesus Christ, it has to be operating under a spirit other than the Holy Spirit. One of the things that can be said about several of the cults is that they seek to bring Jesus down to being just an ordinary man. This is the problem with the Jehovah's Witnesses. Since Mormons have the doctrine of eternal progression, it simply means that Jesus was a created being, once a man, but now has become God. He has gotten ahead of us in the eternal progression. Not only does the doctrine of eternal progression affect God, it also affects Jesus Christ.

The Bible clearly teaches that Jesus is God. This is the basis of the Trinity doctrine, that there are three beings that work together as a unity. These beings are eternal.

Looking more closely at the Mormon doctrine, it teaches that in the very beginning of the earth, God created a large group of spirits. Among the spirits were the Devil and Jesus Christ. All men were spirit beings, gathered around God. God asked the spirits how he could safely usher them all into heaven. The Devil spoke up and said, "If I were given authority over one-third of them I would force them to serve God." Jesus said, "Oh, no, Father. I would teach them to love and worship you." At this point Jesus began to get ahead of us in the eternal progression. There are several serious doctrinal problems here. Can we

---

14 Acts 4:12.

believe, and does the Bible teach, that Jesus is the same age spiritually as all other men? Does the Bible teach that Jesus and the Devil are really brothers: Did Jesus become God just because he was a little smarter than the Devil? Is it true that Jesus is a created God? What does the Bible say?

First, the Bible says that Jesus created all things. "In the beginning was the Word, and the Word was with God, and the Word was God. The same was in the beginning with God. All things were made by him; and without him was not anything made that hath been made."[15] The Bible teaching is that Jesus was God from the very beginning, not that he became God later. In fact, it says that Jesus created everything that has been made. In Colossians it says:

> For by him were all things created, that are in heaven, and that are in earth, visible and invisible, whether they be thrones, or dominions, or principalities, or powers: all things were created by him, and for him: And he is before all things, and by him all things consist. And he is the head of the body, the church: who is the beginning, the firstborn from the dead; that in all things he might have the pre-eminence.[16]

On the basis of such scripture, is it possible to believe a story that says God created a mass of spirits and Jesus was among them? It is clearly stated that Jesus created all things that are in heaven and earth. It also makes clear that Jesus was before all things. Some have argued that since Colossians 1:15 says Jesus was the firstborn of all creation, this meant that Jesus was a created being. It is doubtful that this is its meaning. The very passage says Christ created all things.

Here again we find that not only do they have an incorrect view of God, they seek to bring Jesus down to being a man. This is called anthropomorphizing Jesus, that is, bringing God down into being a man. When a religious body has done such, they have violated the spirit and words of John: "That all may honor the Son, even as they honor the Father. He that honoreth not the Son honoreth not the Father that sent him."[17] The church is built upon Jesus Christ as the Divine Son of God. Mormonism denies this basic doctrine and contradicts clear Bible teaching.

---

15 John 1:1-3.

16 Colossians 1:16-18.

17 John 5:23.

The Virgin Birth of Christ

One of the complications that the doctrine of eternal progression beings upon the Latter-day Saint Church is the virgin birth of Christ. Since the whole order of creation is based upon the act of procreation, they must somehow involve Christ also in this system.

Here again it is a matter of bringing Jesus down to man's level. Brigham Young, the second President of the Mormon Church said: "Now, remember from this time forth, and forever, That Jesus Christ was not begotten by the Holy Ghost."[18] Yet the Bible says, "Now in the sixth month the angel Gabriel was sent from God unto a city of Galilee, named Nazareth, to a virgin betrothed to a man whose name was Joseph...."[19] When the angel told Mary that she would carry a baby, she replied, "How shall this be, seeing I know not a man? And the angel answered and said unto her, the Holy Spirit shall come upon thee, and the power of the Most High shall overshadow thee...."[20]

It is interesting that with the exception of the place of Christ's birth, the Book of Mormon agrees with the Biblical account. Christ was born in Bethlehem.

> And behold, he shall be born of Mary, at Jerusalem which is the land of our forefathers, she being a virgin, a precious and chosen vessel, who shall be overshadowed and conceive by the power of the Holy Ghost, and bring forth a son, yea, even the Son of God.[21]

Yet Joseph Fielding Smith, the recent Prophet and Revelator of the Mormon Church said, "They tell us the Book of Mormon stated that Jesus was begotten of the Holy Ghost. I challenge that statement. The Book of Mormon teaches no such thing. Neither does the Bible. It is true that there is one passage that states so, but we must consider it in the light of other passages with which it is in conflict."[22]

---

18 Young, *Journal of Discourses*, 1:51.

19 Luke 1:26-27.

20 *Ibid.*, 1:34-35.

21 The Book of Mormon, Alma 7:10.

22 Joseph Fielding Smith, *Doctrines of Salvation*, 3 vols., comp. Bruce B. McConkie (Salt Lake City, Utah: Bookcraft, 1956), 1:19

The Mormon Apostle, Orson Pratt, said:

> The fleshly body of Jesus required a mother as well as a father. Therefore, the father and mother of Jesus, according to the flesh, must have been associated together in the capacity of husband and wife; hence the Virgin Mary must have been, for the time being, the lawful wife of God the Father; we must use the term lawful wife, because it would be blasphemous in the highest degree to say that He overshadowed her or begat a Saviour unlawfully.... He had a lawful right to overshadow the Virgin Mary in the capacity of a husband, and begat a son, although she was espoused to another; for the law which he gave to govern men and women was not intended to govern Himself, or to prescribe rules for His own conduct. It was also lawful in Him, after having dealt this with Mary to give her to Joseph her espoused husband. Whether God the Father gave Mary to Joseph her espoused husband, for time only or for time and eternity, we are not informed. Inasmuch as God was the first husband to her, it may be that he only gave her to be the wife of Joseph while in the mortal state, and that He intended after the resurrection to take her as His wife in eternity.[23]

How can we accept such teaching when we read in the Bible, "And Joseph arose from his sleep, and did as the angel of the Lord commanded him, and took her as his wife; and kept her a virgin until she gave birth to a Son: and he called His name Jesus."[25]

Yet, Brigham Young explained the birth of Christ as follows: "The birth of the Saviour was as natural as are the birth of our children: It was the result of natural action. He partook of flesh and blood—was begotten of His Father, as we were of our fathers."[25]

It is quite evident that there is a drastic contradiction between what the Bible says and what the Mormon Church teaches. We know that God is not a god of confusion, so we must conclude that the supposed prophets are not prophets at all, but rather are imposters.

In a sermon at the Tabernacle in Salt Lake City, on April 9, 1852, Brigham Young said:

> I have given you a few leading items upon this subject, but a great deal more remains to be told. Now remember from this time forth, and forever, that Jesus Christ was not begotten by the Holy Ghost. I will repeat a little anec-

---

23 Orson Pratt, *The Seer*, p. 158, as cited with photo reprint by Jerald Tanner and Sandra Tanner, *Mormonism—Shadow or Reality?*, Enl. ed. (Salt Lake City, Utah: Modern Microfilm, 1972), p. 261.

24 Matthew 1:24-25, New American Standard Version.

25 Young, *Journal of Discourses*, 8:115.

dote. I was in conversation with a certain learned professor upon the subject, when I replied, to this idea—"If the Son was begotten by the Holy Ghost, it would be very dangerous to baptize and confirm females, and give the Holy Ghost to them, lest he should beget children, to be palmed upon the Elders by the people, bringing the Elders into great difficulties."[26]

Such teachings verge on blasphemy, if they are not actually such. Sometimes one might wonder if the church today still holds such ideas. A quotation from a recent news article shows this to be true.

> Outburst after outburst of delighted laughter filled the Tabernacle Saturday afternoon as the fourth session of the 143rd annual Conference of the Church of Jesus Christ of Latter-day Saints drew to a close.
>
> The speaker was Elder LeGrand Richards of the Council of Twelve Apostles, well-known for his missionary activities.
>
> Describing an experience he once had in the mission field, Elder Richards told of speaking to a large gathering of clergymen.
>
> *Addresses Gathering*
>
> "I explained to them the difference between reformation and restoration," Elder Richards said. "Then, when I finished my remarks, one of them stood up and said, 'Mr. Richards, we've been told you believe God had a wife. Would you please explain this.'
>
> "I think he thought he had me," said Elder Richards. The audience in the Tabernacle began to chuckle. "I retorted that I didn't see how God could have a Son if He didn't have a wife."
>
> *Proper Answer?*
>
> The Tabernacle audience's chuckle grew to a full roar of laughter as Elder Richards turned to President Harold B. Lee, seated near the podium, to ask if this was a proper answer.
>
> President Lee nodded.[27]

So, still today, the Mormon Church persists in teaching that Jesus was not born of the Virgin Mary, but that God came down and slept with her. It is sickening to think that God would come down and so encroach upon the rights of Joseph. Such teachings are outright blasphemy. According to Jesus, Joseph and Mary would have been living in adultery, for Mary would have been the wife of God, who could visit her when He pleased. To teach such is paganism in the extreme. Even pagans have a higher concept of their gods than to suggest that their morals were lower than man's.

---

26 *Ibid.*, 1:51

27 "Apostle's Humor Draws Laughter," *The Salt Lake Tribune*, 8 April, 1973.

The very basis of Christianity is the Virgin Birth and the Deity of Christ. To deny these facts makes Jesus just a man—in fact, an illegitimate son of God—born from an illicit relationship with another man's espoused wife.

Here again, we have not only a false doctrine, but a very corrupt doctrine that belittles Jesus and His Father.

The Sacrament (Lord's Supper) Elements

One of the issues that is often raised by the Latter-day Saint missionaries is Christian baptism. The Mormon teaching insists upon the strict adherence to the Bible teaching on baptism by total immersion in water for the remission of sin. They base their argument on the clear commands of Christ and his apostles as well as their repeated example. The missionaries are quick to point out such passages as Mark 1:9-10 and Matthew 28:19, and they are right. They are absolutely correct about the mode of baptism. The question that comes to mind, though, is what about the Lord's Supper? Matthew says, "But I say unto you, I will not drink henceforth of the fruit of the vine, until that day when I drink it new with you in my Father's kingdom."[28] Here when Jesus instituted the Lord's Supper He used the fruit of the vine. The Apostle Paul, while teaching about the Lord's Supper in I Corinthians, said Jesus commanded us to observe this simple feast. The Mormons do not use the fruit of the vine, but use water in the communion cup. Is it consistent to insist on obedience in baptism and not on obedience in the Lord's Supper? Of course this puts the Mormons on the spot; how can they explain the need for following the example and command of Jesus in baptism and ignoring it in communion?

The Doctrine and Covenants says in the Word of Wisdom:

> That inasmuch as any man drinketh wine or strong drink among you, behold it is not good, neither meet in the sight of your Father, only in assembling yourselves together to offer up your sacraments before him. And, behold, this should be wine, yea, pure wine of the grape of the vine, of your own make.[29]

---

[28] Matthew 26:29.

[29] Doctrine and Covenants 89:5-6.

Here again we have another instance of the Mormon Church not following the Bible or their own scriptures. It is as though they were condemned out of their own mouths. It shows how totally inconsistent their teachings really are.

Many excuses have been given for this change of doctrine. It has been said that when the Mormons first came to Utah the enemies polluted their wine that was used for communion so as to make them afraid to use it. Some said they were afraid it was poisoned. That might have been a good excuse for a year or two, but grapes grow in Utah today, and it is possible to buy grape juice that is pure from many of their own stores.

One of Jesus' last wishes was that we do these simple things in his memory. To willingly violate his wish would seem to indicate a lack of concern for His will. Again, we find one of the very basic teachings of Jesus and the Bible violated. Can we believe that this is really the restored Church? Is it not one of the most currupt in doctrine of any today?

The High Priesthood

In the Mormon Church many can hold the office of High Priest. The basis of their theology of having thousands of High Priests is baffling. In the Old Testament there was only one High Priest at a time. Aaron was the first High Priest and his sons after him. It would have been unthinkable for there to have been more than one. It would be like having two Presidents in the United States. There were many priests, but only one held the High Priesthood at a time. Another did not take over until the previous High Priest had died.

Today, in the church we read about in our Bible, we find a High Priest.

> Now in the things which we have spoken this is the sum: We have such an high priest, who is set on the right hand of the throne of the Majesty in the heavens; A minister of the sanctuary, and of the true tabernacle, which the Lord pitched, and not man.[30]

Jesus is the High Priest of the church. To have another claim the office, whether by his own decision or to be given the office by another, is to usurp the position that is held today by Jesus Christ.

---

30 Hebrews 8:1-2.

The High Priest was to offer sacrifices for the sins of the people. Not just one high priest, but every high priest was to offer sacrifices for sins. "For every high priest taken from among men is ordained for men in things pertaining to God, that he may offer both gifts and sacrifices for sins."[31] The high priest's job was to offer sacrifices for sins. The question that should be asked of the high priests is, "What sacrifices do they offer for sins?" The Bible says that every high priest is to offer sacrifices for sins. The Bible's statement is quite clear and easily understood; that is, Jesus paid for all sins. What sacrifice could any other priest offer for sin, than the one that has already been offered.

Here is a serious theological problem. It is evident that the Mormon Church is teaching a doctrine contrary to the Bible. Quite apparently the Mormon Church has taught thousands to usurp this office. Many men are claiming to hold an office that belongs only to Jesus Christ.

Baptism For The Dead

In the days of Joseph Smith there were many live issues that were heatedly discussed in the churches. When we read sermons of this era, often we find mention of some of these issues. Baptism for the dead was one of these subjects, along with others, such as preaching to the spirits in prison, and how many heavens there really were.

Since Joseph Smith was a prophet, and prophets have all the answers, he began to teach that a person could be baptized by proxy for someone that had already died. He based this teaching upon the verse of scripture in I Corinthians that says, "Else what shall they do which are baptized for the dead, if the dead rise not at all? why are they then baptized for the dead?"[32]

It would be foolish to say that this scripture was easy to understand. Many church leaders have offered their interpretation of it. The question we need to ask is, does it teach that we can be baptised for dead people by proxy?

A careful examination will show that it says "they do," not "we

---

31 *Ibid.*, 5:1.

32 I Corinthians 15:29

do." If Paul had been practicing baptism for the dead he would have said "we," not "they." It is apparent then that Paul was not practicing it, but the very people who taught that there was no resurrection were also teaching that someone who had died could be baptized by proxy. Paul is pointing out how foolish such a practice was.

Another explanation could also be given. It is apparent that one is baptized because of death. If we didn't ever die, we wouldn't need to be baptized at all. Baptism pictures not only a death, but a resurrection. Since these folks didn't believe in the resurrection, Paul points out that we are really baptized because of death. If there is no resurrection from death, why be baptized?

One rule of interpretation of scripture is that we cannot interpret a hazy passage of scripture in such a way as to contradict a clear passage. Such would be the case here, if we were to understand that Paul is teaching that people who have died in sin can still be saved by a proxy baptism. This would contradict such passages as, "And as it is appointed unto men once to die, but after this the judgment."[33] Jesus clearly taught in the parable of the rich man and Lazarus that after death one's state was sealed.

> There was a certain rich man, which was clothed in purple and fine linen, and fared sumptuously every day: And there was a certain beggar named Lazarus, which was laid at his gate full of sores, And desiring to be fed with the crumbs which fell from the rich man's table: moreover the dogs came and licked his sores. And it came to pass, that the beggar died, and was carried by the angels into Abraham's bosom: the rich man also died, and was buried; And in hell he lift up his eyes, being in torment, and seeth Abraham afar off, and Lazarus in his bosom. And he cried and said, Father Abraham, have mercy on me, and send Lazarus, that he may dip the tip of his finger in water, and cool my tongue; for I am tormented in this flame. But Abraham said, Son, remember that thou in thy lifetime receivest thy good things, and likewise Lazarus evil things: but now he is comforted, and thou art tormented. And beside all this, between us and you there is a great gulf fixed: so that they which would pass from hence to you cannot; neither can they pass to us, that would come from thence.[34]

That would have been a wonderful time for Jesus to tell the world about the second chance, or baptism for the dead. But no,

---

[33] Hebrews 9:27.

[34] Luke 16:19-26.

Jesus doesn't say a word. Why? It is apparent that after death comes the judgment.

The most crushing blow comes to this false doctrine from the Mormon's own scripture, The Book of Mormon. One of the reasons it is so difficult to believe Joseph Smith wrote the Book of Mormon is his apparent unfamiliarity with it. Joseph Smith's later revelations contradict his earlier ones, seeming to indicate he was not familiar with them. Here is a good example, for the Book of Mormon says:

> For behold, this life is the time for men to prepare to meet God; yea, behold the day of this life is the day for men to perform their labors. And now, as I said unto you before, as ye have had so many witnesses, therefore, I beseech of you that ye do not procrastinate the day of your repentance until the end; for after this day of life, which is given us to prepare for eternity, behold, if we do not improve our time while in this life, then cometh the night of darkness wherein there can be no labor performed. Ye cannot say, when ye are brought to that awful crisis, that I will repent, that I will return to my God. Nay, ye cannot say this; for that same spirit which doth possess your bodies at the time that ye go out of this life, that same spirit will have power to possess your body in that eternal world. For behold, if ye have procrastinated the day of your repentance even until death, behold, ye have become subjected to the spirit of the devil, and he doth seal you his; therefore, the Spirit of the Lord hath withdrawn from you and hath no place in you, and the devil hath all power over you; and this is the final state of the wicked.[35]

So the Book of Mormon clears up the matter quite well for the Mormons. When a person dies outside of Jesus he is sealed to Satan for all eternity and that is the final state of the wicked.

This is another evidence that the Latter-day Saint Church does not go by the Bible or the Book of Mormon. According to the teaching of their own books, all the geneology work that they do and all the temple baptisms are a useless waste of time. It is not uncommon for Mormons to have been baptized thirty, forty, or even fifty times for their dead relatives. It is a shame that they have wasted so much time studying geneologies and getting wet for nothing. It is because baptism for the dead is of no value that Paul warns about wasting time on endless geneologies. "But avoid foolish questions, and geneologies, and contentions, and strivings about the law; for they are unprofitable and vain."[36] Cer-

---

35 The Book of Mormon, Alma 34:32-35.

36 Titus 3:9.

tainly Paul could not have made such a statement if baptism for the dead were valid.

So again we have found that the Mormon church doctrine just does not measure up to the close examination that we must give our teachings. We find inconsistencies, contradictions, and outright falsehood throughout this doctrine of hope for those who have whiled away their day of grace until it is too late.

Heavenly Marriage

Two doctrines help to keep the Mormon people in line. These are the doctrines of celestial marriage and sealing of families together. If one does not perform these works in one of the temples they may lose their families for all eternity.

Unless a Mormon person keeps his life in line with church doctrines he cannot get into the temple to perform these works for eternity. It is a real mark of social attainment as well as spiritual attainment to be married in the temple. In order to get into the temple one must have a recommendation from his bishop, who is the equivalent of the preacher in the ordinary congregation. The bishop is not to give this recommendation if the person drinks coffee, tea, or alcoholic beverages, smokes, is not faithful, does not have his tithes paid up to date, and so forth. Therefore, it is a way to keep the people under the subjection of the church. One will think twice about being separated from his wife; maybe someone else would have her, or he would be separated from his children for eternity. So the pressure is put on.

The sorrow about it all is that the Bible teaches that there will be no marriage in heaven. This is clearly stated in three of the four gospels, by Christ Himself. "For in the resurrection they neither marry, nor are given in marriage, but are as the angels of God in heaven."[37]

We will not be married, like people; but like angels, not married at all. Isn't it strange how mixed up people can get things when they seek to play god?

Yes, in heaven we will know our loved ones. The Bible teaches that it will be so. But we will leave behind many of the things that

---

[37] Matthew 22:30. See also Mark 12:25 and Luke 20:35.

we know in this earthly state, and one of the things we will leave behind is marriage. I suppose that to a religion oriented around sex this is a tragic thought.

The Gospel of Jesus Preached by Adam, Enoch, Noah, Abraham, and Others

At first this may seem like a rather harmless doctrine. Yet is falsehood ever really harmless? The real question is, "Does it measure up to the truth?" Did the Old Testament people understand and preach the same gospel story that we preach? Were these folks saved in exactly the same way we are?

The Book of Mormon teaches that the people that came to America preached Jesus Christ and baptized people who believed.

> And he commandeth all men that they must repent, and be baptized in his name, having perfect faith in the Holy One of Israel, or they cannot be saved in the kingdom of God. And if they will not repent and believe in his name, and be baptized in his name, and endure to the end, they must be damned; for the Lord God, the Holy One of Israel, has spoken it.[38]

A similar statement is made again by Nephi:

> And now, if the Lamb of God, he being holy, should have need to be baptized by water, to fulfil all righteousness, O then, how much more need have we, being unholy, to be baptized, yea, even by water! And now, I would ask of you, my beloved brethren, wherein the Lamb of God did fulfil all righteousness in being baptized by water?...[39]

The problem with these passages from the Book of Mormon is that they were supposedly written about 550 B.C. Are we to believe that they had the same message to preach then that we do now? What does the New Testament scripture say about this matter?

The New Testament teaches quite clearly that the prophets did not receive the same promises that we do.

> Of which salvation the prophets have enquired and searched diligently, who prophesied of the grace that should come unto you: Searching what, or what manner of time the Spirit of Christ which was in them did signify, when it testified beforehand the sufferings of Christ, and the glory that should follow. Unto whom it was revealed, that not unto themselves, but unto us they did minister the things, which are now reported unto you by them that

---

38 The Book of Mormon, II Nephi 9:23-24.

39 *Ibid.*, 31:5-6.

> have preached the gospel unto you with the Holy Ghost sent down from heaven; which things the angels desire to look into.[40]

Paul puts the matter even more clearly when he says:

> Unto me, who am less than the least of all saints, was this grace given, to preach unto the Gentiles the unsearchable riches of Christ; and to make all men see what is the dispensation of the mystery which for ages hath been hid in God who created all things.[41]

The mystery of the gospel was not fully known before Jesus came to earth. We have absolutely no record of it being preached, other than the prophets looking ahead and prophesying that it would come some day in the future.

The book of Romans also indicates that Jesus' salvation was not fully understood till after His death. Even the apostles didn't know what was going on until after the Holy Spirit came upon them. "Now to him that is of power to stablish you according to my gospel, and the preaching of Jesus Christ, according to the revelation of the mystery, which was kept secret since the world began."[42]

So there we have it again. The mystery of salvation through Jesus was not preached until after His resurrection. Even the work of John the Baptist was only one of a "way-preparer."

Here again is an indication that the Book of Mormon was not really written as early as it claims to have been. It is really easy to know all the details of events after they happen. It would have been an easy thing to have written the Book of Mormon after the events had taken place, pretending that it was really an ancient book. This is very good evidence that the book is not nearly as old as Joseph Smith said it was.

Beyond this, the Bible clearly shows that this doctrine of salvation being preached in the name of Jesus in Old Testament days is false. It is another proof that the Mormon system is not of God.

Supposed Cursed Races

The doctrine of cursed races was a part of Mormon teaching from the beginning of the L.D.S. church until June 9, 1978. At

---

40 I Peter 1:10-13.

41 Ephesians 3:8-9.

42 Romans 16:25.

that time a pronouncement was made by President Spencer W. Kimball which said, "...all worthy male members of the church may be ordained to the priesthood without regard for race or color."[43]

Below is a refutation of this absurd doctrine, so long held by the L.D.S. church and how it came to be changed. (The following material was written in 1975. Three years later the doctrine was changed.)

The doctrine was taken from the statements made in the Pearl of Great Price, Book of Abraham and statements from the Book of Mormon. According to these sources the Negro and American Indian had dark skin because of their sins.[44] This is a very serious accusation because it places a slur upon every black person.

The doctrine is that because people were sinful in the preexistence, God placed them in black skins here as a punishment. This would lead one to have serious doubts about a black person's trustworthiness. In fact, this doctrine has been interpreted so as to not let one Negro have a place of leadership in the Mormon church. A white boy of twelve years of age can hold a higher office than a grown Negro man can.

The passage in the Book of Abraham says, "Now, Pharaoh being of that lineage by which he could not have the right of Priesthood, notwithstanding the Pharaohs would fain claim it from Noah, through Ham, therefore my father was led away by their idolatry."[45] This passage has been interpreted by the prophets of the Mormon church to mean Negroes were cursed by God. Joseph Fielding Smith, recent Prophet of the Latter-day Saint Church stated:

> Not only was Cain called upon to suffer, but because of his wickedness he became the father of an inferior race. A curse was placed upon him, and that curse has been continued through his lieage, and must do so while time endures.[46]

In another place he says:

> There is a reason why one man is born black and with other disadvantages,

---

[43] Deseret News, June 9, 1978, Page 1A.

[44] II Nephi 5:21-22; Alma 3:6; Abraham 1:21-27.

[45] Pearl of Great Price, Abraham 1:27.

[46] Joseph Fielding Smith, *The Way To Perfection*, (Salt Lake City, Utah: Deseret Press), p. 101.

while another is born white with great advantages. The reason is that we once had an estate before we came here, and were obedient, more or less, to the laws that were given us there. Those who were faithful in all things there received greater blessings here, and those who were not faithful received less.[47]

In a letter dated April 10, 1963, Joseph Fielding Smith says:

According to the doctrine of the Church, the Negro because of some condition of unfaithfulness in the spirit—or pre-existence, was not valiant and hence was not denied the mortal probation, but denied the blessing of the priesthood.[48]

Brigham Young, second prophet of the Mormon Church, stated:

Cain slew his brother. Cain might have been killed, and that would have put a termination to the line of human beings. This was not to be, and the Lord put a mark upon him, which is the flat nose and black skin....[49]

Can these serious accusations, directed towards a whole race of people, be substantiated by the Bible? Since the race problem is so current, with so many side effects possible, it would be helpful to show what the Bible really does say about the Negro race.

So often the Bible has been used as a crutch to keep the black race down. People have looked within its pages to find sanction for slavery, racial injustices, and discrimination. This doctrine, held by the Latter-day Saint Church, is a relic of the ignorant past, a definite indication that they do not have a prophet in their midst.

Two passages of scripture have been used as proof texts to support their contention that the black race is inferior, due to an act of God. These two passages of scripture are Genesis 4:15 and Genesis 9:20-27. Due to a hazy and faulty interpretation of these two passages, "Christians" have thought themselves justified in keeping the black race in bondage; at least they sought to justify their doing so.

The first passage deals with the "mark of Cain." It does not say what the mark was, but it has been affirmed by many religious leaders of various faiths that God turned Cain black as a curse for

---

47 Joseph Fielding Smith, *Doctrines of Salvation, 1:61.*

48 Jerald Tanner and Sandra Tanner, *Mormonism—Shadow or Reality?* 1964, ed., p. 296.

49 Young, *Journal of Discourses,* 7:290-91.

his sin of murder. A program was aired on KSXX radio station in Salt Lake City, discussing the problem of Cain and what his curse meant. The discussion at times was quite heated. Finally a lady called in who was apparently an older Negro woman. She said, "We think God turned Cain white." She had a very good point, and there is easily as much proof for her point of view as there is for the Mormons'. It could have as easily been that God turned Cain white, rather than black. The passage certainly does not prove Cain was turned a different color at all.

The second passage mentions the curse that Noah put on his grandson, Canaan, because Ham saw his father's nakedness. The obvious fault in reasoning here is that Ham is said to mean "black skinned." There is a similar word in Hebrew that can mean "black skinned," but basically the word "Ham" (חָם) means "father-in-law." It is very, very doubtful that Ham's name meant "black skinned." As a Bible scholar, I would hate to insist that it did mean such. Beyond this, the curse was not placed on Ham at all, but upon his son, Canaan.

The evidence seems to indicate that the Negro races are not of Canaan at all. T.B. Maston says:

> It is generally agreed that the Canaanites, descendants of Canaan, were not black. In the main, they moved into Asia Minor and at least as far east as the Tigris and Euphrates valley. Other descendants of Ham went south into Africa, but not the Canaanites, upon whom the curse was at least specially pronounced. Ryle suggests that "the application of this clause to the African races is an error of interpretation." Similarly, Marcus Dods concludes, "Canaan being thus selected, the fulfillment of the curse must not be looked for in the other descendants of Ham, and still less in the Negro races." Pieters likewise says that even if the Negroes be conceded to be the sons of Ham, they are certainly not descendants of Canaan, and these only are under the curse.[50]

We must conclude that God never has cursed the Negro people at all. Ignorant Protestants, in a Southern culture, sought to justify their keeping other humans in bondage by scripture passages of doubtful meaning at best. The Mormons, while in Missouri, picked up this teaching and while most Protestants have gotten their eyes open to the truth, the Mormons continue to hold to a doctrine that is not only ignorant, but debasing to a

---

50 T. B. Maston, *The Bible and Race* (Nashville, Tenn.: Broadman Press, 1962), p. 112.

great segment of our country's population.

If there had ever been a curse placed on the Negroes it would have been removed in Christ, for the scripture says:

> For as many of you as have been baptized into Christ have put on Christ. There is neither Jew nor Greek, there is neither bond nor free, there is neither male nor female: for ye are all one in Christ Jesus. And if ye be Christ's then are ye Abraham's seed, and heirs according to the promise.[51]

Nationalities are bridged, races and social distinctions are spanned, and economic and servitude lines are crossed when one comes into Christ. This passage is so clear that it must of necessity take preference over ones of such doubtful interpretation as those mentioned in Genesis.

The Colossian letter speaks even more clearly about this matter when it says:

> ...and have put on the new man, which is renewed in knowledge after the image of him that created him: where there is neither Greek nor Jew, circumcision nor uncircumcision, Barbarian, Scythian, bond nor free: but Christ is all, and in all.[52]

This passage also makes it very clear that Christ breaks down all barriers of race and culture.

It is likely that several people who came into the church in its beginning were of the black race. This has been almost entirely overlooked by those who reject their black brothers. What about Simeon who was called Niger?[53] It seems as likely, or much more so, that he was black than Cain or Canaan were. Yet he was prominent in the church at Antioch. It is also likely that the Ethiopian Eunuch was of a dark-skinned race. He was received into the church without question by Phillip the Evangelist.[54] Men from "every nation under heaven"[55] were received into the church on the Day of Pentecost. We can remember the words of God to Peter when Peter was told to "rise, kill and eat."[56] Peter didn't want to touch the unclean animals, but God told him to do so.

---

51 Galatians 3:27-29.

52 Colossians 3:10-11.

53 Acts 13:1.

54 *Ibid.*, 8:26-39.

55 *Ibid.*, 2:5.

56 *Ibid.*, 10:13.

Peter later said in reference to this revelation from God, "Of a truth I perceive that God is no respecter of persons: but in every nation he that feareth him, and worketh righteousness, is acceptable to him."[57]

Another passage of scripture that speaks clearly about the race issue is also found in Acts. "And he made of one every nation of men to dwell on all the face of the earth, having determined their appointed seasons, and the bounds of their habitation."[58] Was the Apostle speaking the truth? Has God made all nations one in Christ? It would certainly appear so. Christ died for all mankind. Heaven is prepared for all mankind. God created all mankind. God has not placed any biological blocks between the races for they can marry and raise children. The Bible repeatedly stresses that any who wishes may be saved. That God does not want any to perish is a clear teaching of scripture. Those who are in Christ Jesus are one body, His church.

Jesus spoke directly about racial prejudice in his ministry. The Jews were very prejudiced against the Samaritans. They would travel around their country rather than to pass through it. They would have no social interaction with them. They preferred not even to do business with them. Their racial pride was very similar to what we see often today in America.

When a certain lawyer asked Jesus what he should do to inherit eternal life, Christ answered with another question.

> ...What is written in the law? how readest thou? And he answering said, Thou shalt love the Lord thy God with all thy heart, and with all thy soul, and with all thy strength, and with all thy mind; and thy neighbor as thyself. And he said unto him, Thou hast nswered right: this do, and thou shalt live. But he, willing to justify himself, said unto Jesus, And who is my neighbor?[59]

Jesus then told the story of the man who was injured and a priest and a Levite passed by, while the despised Samaritan stopped and helped the man who was hurt. Jesus here pictures the despised race as being more acceptable than those they counted worthy of honor. Jesus shows the Samaritan as being the one pleasing to God. Might it be so today? Could it be that those who feel they are

---

57 *Ibid.*, 10:35.

58 *Ibid.*, 17:26.

59 Luke 10:26-29.

the elect of God, the special favored race, are not as acceptable as those sometimes considered inferior.

Jesus later took time to win the Samaritan woman. She was forgiven and became the evangelizer of her city.[60] Peter and John went to Samaria to preach and impart spiritual gifts to those who were won by Philip.[61] This is clear proof that in Christ racial prejudice was stripped away.

Several passages of scripture teach that the Gospel message is to be taken to all the earth, without racial distinction. Our great commission teaches, "Go ye therefore, and teach all nations, baptizing them in the name of the Father, and of the Son, and of the Holy Ghost."[62] When the gospel was first preached by Peter he said, "For the promise is unto you, and to your children, and to all that are afar off, even as many as the Lord our God shall call."[63]

Here again we find the Mormon Church on the wrong side of truth. Not just once do we find it so, but again and again. The conclusion seems warranted that the Mormon Church has more error in it than any other false religious body that claims to be "Christian." It is puzzling how important, intelligent men have been kept in the ignorance of the system. The only explanation is that they have not checked their doctrine. Either they do not know their doctrine, or they have not carefully checked to see if it is correct.

It is likely that the Mormon Church will some day, before too long, change this doctrine. The recent prophet of the Mormon Church, Harold B. Lee, said, and I paraphrase, "...it's only a matter of time before the Negro will achieve full status in the church.... The Negro will achieve full status and we're just waiting for that time.[64] In other words, Where is God? And why doesn't He get along with it and help them out of a bad doctrine? Can we really believe in such a God?

So we see the relics of the false doctrine of the past still perpetrated by the Mormon system, which is slow to change. It is a

---

60 John 4:7-42.

61 Acts 8:14-17.

62 Matthew 28:19.

63 Acts 2:39.

64 *The Salt Lake Tribune*, 24 September, 1972, p. 14B.

church run by extremely old men, whose views are often at least fifty years behind the times. It is apparent that they do not have a hot line to God, or they would have been able to clear up such a problem as this years ago.

The Mormon racial position is in direct contradiction to the Bible. It is a position probably based on racial superstitions, learned from their southern heritage and their stay in Independence, Missouri. The Mormon viewpoint is that of a hundred years ago, a cultural viewpoint, un-Biblical, and as outdated as slavery. It definitely should be abandoned. It not only should be dropped because of scriptural reasons, but because it is an affront to our American way of life today.

And so another false doctrine has been straightened out as of June 9, 1978. How many others need to be changed? Can we trust prophets who are so sure they are right, while all the time they are wrong? The Bible says, "Jesus Christ is the same yesterday and today, yes and forever."[65] "Let them alone; they are blind guides of the blind. And if a blind man guides a blind man, both will fall into a pit."

Polygamy

The Church of Jesus Christ of Latter-day Saints asserts that polygamy is not a current issue with them, and has not been since the declaration of Wilford Woodruff, President of the Church, on October 6, 1890. This is not entirely true. I lived in Salt Lake City for seven years and have known of many polygamists.

The church has not actively encouraged it, nor has it actively sought to stamp it out. When an individual makes an issue of someone being a polygamist, then the polygamist is put out of the church. This has happened many times. Yet today it is estimated that there are thousands in the church practicing polygamy. The group most actively promoting polygamy call themselves "fundamentalists."

An article in *The Ladies Home Journal* in 1967 had the subtitle, "30,000 Cases of Polygamy in Utah."[66] Polygamy's greatest growth has taken place since that time so this number has likely

---

[65] Hebrews 13:8 and Matthew 15:14. N.A.S.V.

[66] Ben Merson, "Husbands With More Than One Wife," *Ladies Home Journal*, June 1967, pp.78-79.

doubled. The author of this article went to Utah and lived among the people, agreeing not to name names or disclose his sources. After working under these conditions for a year he came to the above figure. Now, if polygamy has doubled in Utah since 1970, you can begin to see the extent of the problem today.

Polygamists do not have to hide their polygamy, for they are not prosecuted at all. The excuse for not enforcing the law is that it would flood the welfare rolls beyond endurance. (Utah already has a high rate of welfare recipients.)

In counseling with polygamists one finds all sorts of family problems that arise because of jealousy. A young woman became a member of the Christian Church in Salt Lake City without revealing the fact that she was the wife of a polygamist. The husband of the family felt duty bound to practice polygamy and used as his reason the 132nd section of the Doctrine and Covenants. He said it was a terrible burden to have to practice polygamy. In order for him to take another wife, he had to have the permission of the ones he already had. His "Christian" wife would not give this permission, so he resorted to physical force, during which she received a black eye and a very swollen lip. Later she left him and he took the wife that he was wanting. He insisted that he only practiced polygamy out of duty to please God and insisted that it was a terrible burden. It is unlikely that his motives were as pure as he would have had people think.

Another well known incident involved a man who had seven wives. Each of these wives was young and pretty. Not one of them was the sort of person one might expect them to be, possibly unattractive, lacking in personality, or deficient in some way, persons who would give in to polygamy because they were afraid they would never get a husband if they didn't. Such was not the case. One of the wives was a registered nurse, one taught school, and one was a certified public accountant. Our source of information is a brother of one of the seven wives, who is a sharp business man. His sister is quite pretty and intelligent.

Near the mouth of Little Cottonwood Canyon, near Salt Lake City, lives a man who also has seven wives and more than twenty children. It is common knowledge among the people of the whole area that this family practices polygamy. Several children attend public school together, are nearly the same ages, brothers and sisters, but not twins, sharing the same name and the same father.

In Bountiful, Utah, there is a man with twelve wives and twenty-four children. This case of polygamy is widely known to exist, and nothing is done to seek to stop it.

Some estimate that today in the Salt Lake City area, there are more people practicing polygamy per capita than there were in the days of Brigham Young, before polygamy was outlawed. If the Mormon Church wanted to stop the progress of polygamy they could, for they control the state, politically, economically, and socially.

Polygamy is viewed as being illegal, like breaking the speed limit, but really not offensive to God. Therefore many practice it with a clear conscience since their scripture commands it. In their eyes they are obeying God rather than men.

The passages that endorse polygamy are:

> Verily, thus saith the Lord unto you my servant Joseph, that inasmuch as you have inquired of my hand to know and understand wherein I, the Lord, justified my servants Abraham, Isaac, and Jacob, as also Moses, David and Solomon, my servants, as touching the principle and doctrine of their having many wives and concubines—Behold, and lo, I am the Lord thy God, and will answer thee as touching this matter. Therefore, prepare thy heart to receive and obey the instructions which I am about to give unto you; for all those who have this law revealed unto them must obey the same. For behold, I reveal unto you a new and an everlasting covenant; and if ye abide not that covenant, then are ye damned; for no one can reject this covenant and be permitted to enter into my glory....and he that receiveth a fulness thereof must and shall abide the law, or he shall be damned, saith the Lord God.[67]

Joseph Smith is very wordy under normal circumstances, but seems a little more vague than usual. I would suspect that he is trying to molify Emma Smith, his wife. He needs to be definite, but wants to be a little ambiguous at the same time. A little later in the same section he says:

> Go ye, therefore, and do the works of Abraham; enter ye into my law and ye shall be saved. But if ye enter not into my law ye cannot receive the promise of my Father, which he made unto Abraham. God commanded Abraham, and Sarah give Hagar to Abraham to wife. And why did she do it? Because this was the law; and from Hagar sprang many people. This, therefore, was fulfilling, among other things, the promises.[68]

---

67 Doctrine and Covenants 132:1-4, 6.

68 *Ibid.*, 132:32-34.

It is quite clear that Joseph is commanded to do the works of Abraham and that was that God commanded Abraham to be a polygamist. I don't know how it could be read differently. Yet there is more to be said:

> David also received many wives and concubines, and also Solomon and Moses my servants, as also many others of my servants, from the beginning of creation until this time; and in nothing did they sin save in those things which they received not of me. David's wives and concubines were given unto him of me, by the hand of Nathan, my servant, and others of the prophets who had the keys of this power; and in none of these things did he sin against me...I am the Lord thy God, and I gave unto thee, my servant Joseph, an appointment, and restore all things.[69]

Again the message comes through loud and clear. God is supposedly restoring polygamy. In the same section there is a lengthy appeal to Emma Smith to receive this new commandment, with blessings promised to her if she does and curses if she does not. As a part of this Joseph is promised many wives.

> But if she [Emma] will not abide this commandment, then shall my servant Joseph do all things for her, even as he hath said; and I will bless him and multiply him and give unto him an hundredfold in this world, of fathers and mothers, brothers and sisters, houses and lands, wives and children, and crowns of eternal lives in the eternal worlds.[70]

The climax comes when he says:

> And again, as pertaining to the law of the priesthood—if any man espouse a virgin, and desire to espouse another, and the first give her consent, and if he espouse the second, and they are virgins, and have vowed to no other man, then is he justified; he cannot commit adultery for they are given unto him, for he cannot commit adultery with that that belongeth unto him and to no one else. And if he have ten virgins given unto him by this law, he cannot commit adultery, for they belong to him, and they are given unto him; therefore is he justified.[71]

So there we have it; a new and everlasting covenant that lasted until the United States Militia put the pressure on a future prophet of the Latter-day Saint Church. Then he received word to do away with the "everlasting covenant." But today, slowly but surely, it is coming back, or should we say, has come back, with renewed vigor.

---

69 *Ibid.*, 132:38-40.

70 *Ibid.*, 132:55.

71 *Ibid.*, 132:61-62.

How anyone could deny that the major emphasis of the 132nd section of Doctrine and Covenants is polygamy is beyond imagination. It is clearly taught.

In the beginning polygamy was not the rule. When God created Adam and Eve he didn't make Adam many wives. If he had wanted people to multiply on the earth, and this was his reason for giving polygamy, why not make Adam several wives. But the command was, "Therefore shall a man leave his father and his mother, and shall cleave unto his wife: and they shall be one flesh."[72] Man was to cleave to his wife, singular.

Later when polygamy became common it was usually associated with trouble. A little research will show almost every case of polygamy in the Bible is attended with trouble. Abraham had a serious problem with Sarah and Hagar, even making it necessary to put Hagar out of his house. The two nations that came from this polygamist union have hated each other ever since. The Jews and the Arabs are still fighting.

David got himself into trouble, not only with Bathsheba, but his children hated each other, murdered each other, and one of his own sons defiled his wives upon Mount Zion, in the sight of all Israel.

Solomon's wives turned his heart away from God. Both David and Solomon died relatively young men, probably in their early sixties. It is not suggested that these men were lost, since they lived in a time when they didn't have as clear a revelation of God's will as we do today.

But today we have clear teaching in the Bible that church leaders are to only have one wife, not to be polygamists. "A bishop then must be blameless, the husband of one wife, vigilant, sober, of good behaviour,...Let the deacons be the husbands of one wife, ruling their children and their own houses well."[73] Most Bible scholars believe that there was some polygamy in the days of the early church, but none of these were to have places of leadership in the church.

A similar set of instructions is given to Titus, for him to go by

---

[72] Genesis 2:24.

[73] I Timothy 3:2 & 12.

in choosing church leaders. "For this cause left I thee in Crete, that thou shouldest set in order the things that are wanting, and ordain elders in every city, as I had appointed thee: If any be blameless, the husband of one wife..."[74] There is no need for us to misunderstand, for the instruction is given twice. Elders, Bishops, and Deacons are to have only one wife.

Under the section on "The Book of Mormon," it has already been pointed out that the Book of Mormon says no one is to have more than one wife. We must remember that God is not a God of confusion. He is unchanging, the same yesterday, today, and forever.

The Marriage of Jesus

It is often hard to pinpoint just what the official doctrine of the Latter-day Saint Church really is at any one given time. All that can be done is to quote influential leaders of the church and what they have said about their views. A few quotations from some of the leaders of the church on the matter of Christ's marriage will illustrate their views.

> It will be borne in mind that once on a time, there was a marriage in Cana of Galilee; and on a careful reading of that transaction, it will be discovered that no less a person than Jesus Christ was married, on that occasion. If he was never married, his intimacy with Mary and Martha and the other Mary also whom Jesus loved, must have been highly unbecoming and improper to say the best of it.
>
> I will venture to say that if Jesus Christ were now to pass through the most pious countries in Christendom with a train of woman such as used to follow him, fondling about him, combing his hair, annointing him with precious ointment, washing his feet with tears, and wiping them with the hair of their heads and unmarried, or even married, he would be mobbed, tarred, and feathered, and rode not on an ass, but on a rail.[75]

This is a bit of plain blasphemy in print. It is painful to even record it. Yet, such has been the extent of the false doctrine of the Mormon Church. The Mormon Apostle Jedediah Grant commented:

> The grand reason of the burst of public sentiment in anathemas upon Christ and his disciples, causing his crucifixion, was evidently based upon

---

[74] Titus 1:5-6.

[75] Orson Hyde, "Man the Head of Woman—Kingdom of God—The Seed of Christ—Polygamy—Society in Utah," *Journal of Discourses, 4:259.*

polygamy, according to the testimony of the philosophers who rose in that age. A belief in the doctrine of a plurality of wives caused the persecution of Jesus and his followers. We might almost think they were "Mormons."[76]

The Mormon Church does not now actively teach that Jesus was married; however, the doctrines of the Church imply He had at least one wife and possibly more. The highest degree a person can reach in Heaven is called "exaltation" and this is not attainable by an unmarried person. A man and woman must be sealed for time and all eternity by an authorized person in a temple ceremony before exaltation is possible. It would appear from this doctrine that Jesus would have to have been marrried in this manner to fulfill all requirements, to obtain his exaltation, and thus be worthy of returning to the presence of God the Father. The highest attainable goal that an unmarried person can reach is that of a ministering angel. The Mormon doctrine does not teach that Jesus is a ministering angel, but that of a God second only to God the Father. This doctrine, that Christ was married, has been taught by a very high authority, Brigham Young.

They have refused our brethren membership in their lodge, because they are polygamists. Who was the founder of Free-masonery? They can go back as far as Solomon, and there they stop. There is the king who established this high and holy order. Now was he a polygamist, or was he not? If he did believe in monogamy, he did not practice it a great deal, for he had seven hundred wives, and that is more than I have, and he had three hundred concubines, of which I have none that I know of. Yet the whole fraternity throughout Christendom will cry out against this order. "Oh dear, Oh dear, Oh dear," they all cry out; "I am in pain....I am suffering at witnessing the wickedness there is in the land. Here is one of the 'relics' of barbarism." Yes, one of the relics of Adam, of Enoch, of Noah, of Abraham, of Isaac, of Jacob, of Moses, David, Solomon, the Prophets, AND JESUS AND HIS APOSTLES[77]

On July 2, 1899 Apostle George Q. Cannon made the following statement followed by an answer by the President of the Church, Lorenzo Snow. Cannon said:

There are those in this audience who are descendants of the old Twelve Apostles—and shall I say it, yes, DESCENDANTS OF THE SAVIOR HIMSELF. HIS SEED IS REPRESENTED IN THIS BODY OF MEN.

---

[76] Jedediah M. Grant, "Uniformity"; *Journal of Discourses*, 1:346.

[77] Brigham Young, *Deseret News*, 10 Feb. 1867, cited by Ogden Kraut, *Jesus Was Married* (Dugway, Utah: Ogden Kraut, 1970), p. 62.

> Following President Cannon, President Snow arose and said that what Brother Cannon had stated respecting the literal descendants among this company of the old apostles and the Saviour Himself is true—that the Savior's seed is represented in this body of men.[78]

The preceding quotations are only a small sampling of what is written upon the subject of Christ's having been married and a polygamist. One verse of scripture will show the absurdity of such a doctrine. "He was led as a sheep to the slaughter; and as a lamb before his shearer is dumb, so he openeth not his mouth: In his humiliation his judgment was taken away: His generation who shall declare? For his life is taken from the earth."[79]

The Paid Ministry

The work of the Latter-day Saint church is almost entirely by volunteers. This holds true of the officers and leaders of the local Wards right on up through the President of the Church. (The President heads several of the large corporations of the church, for which he receives a handsome salary.) This is reported to be the case with the apostles as well. Yet for the many thousands of people who work for the church, they do so free. We can admire their dedication. Yet is this really good, or is it really God's will?

What it means is that the leaders of the church all must have other occupations to support themselves and the heavy tithing they are expected to give to the church. Therefore the whole movement is led by amateurs. Seldom are people found who really know what they are talking about. Many instances of inadequate counseling, or just plain harmful counseling, and unethical techniques are the result. Many times this has not been an intentional effort to misdirect people, but just the result of incompetent leadership.

One area that shows the lack of trained leadership is funerals. Poor taste, appalling ineptitude, inadequate solace are often experienced by those in grief.

---

78 *Journal of Pres. Rudger Clawson*, pp. 374-375, cited by Ogden Kraut, Jesus Was Married (Dugway, Utah: Ogden Kraut, 1970), p. 97.

79 Acts 8:32-33.

It has been said that in all the years of the Mormon church, they have not yet produced one real theologian. This is probably true. It is all tied in with the unpaid leadership. It makes it impossible to produce and maintain a competent leadership. This basic ignorance of theology is experienced from the newest missionary up through the ranks, even to the apostles.

The Bible is quite plain about the matter of the paid ministry. Jesus had very good reasons for so directing. Paul shows the reasons in his letter to the Corinthian church.

> Who goeth a warfare any time at his own charges? who planteth a vineyard, and eateth not of the fruit thereof? or who feedeth a flock, and eateth not of the milk of the flock? Say I these things as a man? or saith not the law the same also? For it is written in the law of Moses, Thou shalt not muzzle the mouth of the ox that treadeth out the corn. Doth God take care for oxen? Or saith he it altogether for our sakes? For our sakes, no doubt, this is written: that he that ploweth should plow in hope; and that he that thresheth in hope should be partaker of his hope. If we have sown unto you spiritual things, is it a great thing if we shall reap your carnal things? If others be partakers of this power over you, are not we rather? Nevertheless we have not used this power; but suffer all things, lest we should hinder the gospel of Christ. Do ye not know that they which minister about holy things live of the things of the temple? and they which wait at the altar are partakers with the altar? Even so hath the Lord ordained that they which preach the gospel should live of the gospel.[80]

Paul also reminded the Galatian Christians that, "Let him that is taught in the word communicate unto him that teacheth in all good things."[81] This is an obvious teaching of the paid ministry. Paul received wages to preach the gospel. "I robbed other churches, taking wages from them, to do you service."[82]

Here again, is it possible to believe that a church that has no paid ministry is the restored Church of Christ on earth? Don't you want to be a part of a church that has competent, qualified leadership? Remember, Jesus warned about the blind being led by the blind.

Elders and Deacons

The Bible gives clear guidelines as to the qualifications for the elders and deacons in the church. Yet in the Latter-day Saint

---

80 I Corinthians 9:7-14.

81 Galatians 6:6.

82 II Corinthians 11:8.

Church we find that these guidelines are not at all followed. In fact, a boy of twelve years of age can be a deacon in the church, and a young man of sixteen can be an elder. In the light of clear Bible pronouncements on this subject, we wonder how the church can claim to have restored the New Testament church like it was established by the apostles and Christ.

Beyond this, the Mormon Church makes a distinction between the elder and the bishop. The bishop is considered to be a higher office than the elder. We learn from the scriptures that the office of elder and bishop are one and the same thing. Paul uses them interchangeably.

> For this cause left I thee in Crete, that thou shouldest set in order the things that are wanting, and ordain elders in every city, as I have appointed thee: If any be blameless, the husband of one wife, having faithful children not accused of riot or unruly. For a bishop must be blameless...[83]

Here the words elder and bishop are used interchangeably for one and the same office. It stipulates that an elder is to have a wife and children. This is a rather stringent requirement for a sixteen year old boy, hardly ready to shave yet. Of course, Paul didn't mean that sixteen year old boys should be elders. It is just another case of the false teachings of the Latter-day Saint Church.

The Bible teaches that a deacon is to be married. Paul said, "Let the deacons be the husbands of one wife, ruling their children and their own houses well."[84]

Certainly we cannot say that the L.D.S. Church has restored the Bible's teaching about church leadership.

---

83 Titus 1:5-7.

84 I Timothy 3:12.

Chapter X

SUMMARY AND CONCLUSIONS

After almost a life-time of working with Mormons, these are some of the most important things that have been used to win them to Christ. It all must begin with a genuine love for them and a desire to help them to see the wonderful beauty of Jesus Christ and His salvation. It is doubtful that any can be helped without first genuinely loving them.

One must begin with the Bible. A neighbor became convinced that the Mormon Church was wrong, but at the same time lost faith in the Bible, so he went out and got drunk. One must be careful to establish the Bible as God's word, first. Then the careful teacher can proceed to show the error of the Mormon system. Therefore, it is a must to establish the Bible as the Word of God. Begin as is suggested in this book. Prove the accuracy of the Bible, as is done in chapters one and two of this book. The Mormon people have been taught to suspect the Bible's accuracy. They will rejoice to find that it is accurate and dependable.

The comparison that is drawn between the Bible and Book of Mormon should present dramatic proof that the books do not come from the same source. The changes, literary problems, textual problems, present problems that demonstrate that it is not scripture.

Chapter four shows some of the problems of theology that are within the Book of Mormon. It is interesting to notice that the Mormon Church does not go by the Bible or The Book of Mormon.

The Doctrine and Covenants is the real source of many of the false teachings that are found within the Mormon Church today. It has been shown that there are many doctrinal changes, even though the very first section claims that it should and would never be changed. The false doctrines contained within this book certainly are proof that Joseph Smith was not a man of God.

The Pearl of Great Price gives us positive scientific proof that Joseph Smith could not read a foreign language. In fact, how he could take fifty-six characters and translate them into over four thousand words is beyond the imagination. Again, dramatic proof that the Mormon system is not of God.

Part Two of this book shows what the Bible has to say about a prophet of God. All the evidence could be summed up in a few words. Prophets of God have never contradicted the previous prophets. Certainly if Joseph Smith had been a prophet he would not have taught so many false doctrines.

Part Three discusses thirteen doctrinal issues in which Joseph Smith, The Book of Mormon, the Doctrine and Covenants, Pearl of Great Price, and later prophets have taught doctrines contrary to the teachings of Christ and His apostles.

Is the Mormon Church the restored Church of Christ on earth? It is in fact one of the most perverted of churches that claim to be a church of Christ.

We might conclude by quoting the words of Jesus, "For there shall arise false Christs, and false prophets, and shall shew great signs and wonders; insomuch that, if it were possible, they shall deceive the very elect."[1] "Beware of false prophets, which come to you in sheep's clothing, but inwardly they are ravening wolves."[2]

The Apostle John said, "Beloved, believe not every spirit, but try the spirits whether they are of God: because many false prophets are gone out into the world."[3]

---

1 Matthew 24:24.

2 *Ibid.*, 7:5.

3 I John 4:1.

BIBLIOGRAPHY

"Apostle's Humor Draws Laughter." *The Salt Lake Tribune*, 8 April, 1973.

Biblical Archaeology Review. Sept.-Oct. 1980, p. 26.

Cowdry, Davis and Scales. *Who Really Wrote the Book of Mormon?* Santa Anna, CA: Vision House Publishers, 1977.

Everyday Life in Bible Times. National Geographic Society, Washington, D.C., 1967.

Jonas, Larry. *Mormon Claims Examined*. Grand Rapids, MI: Baker Book House, 1961.

"History of Joseph Smith." *Millenial Star*, (April 6, 1861): 23:246-47.

Journal of Pres. Rudger Clawson, pp. 374-375. Cited by Ogden Kraut, *Jesus Was Married*, p. 97. Dugway, Utah: by the author, 1970.

Maston, T. B. The Bible and Race. Nashville, Tenn.: Broadman Press, 1962.

Merson, Ben. "Husbands With More Than One Wife." *Ladies Home Journal*, June, 1967, pp. 78-79.

Miller, H. S. *General Biblical Introduction*. Houghton, New York: The Word-Bearer Press, 1959.

Pratt, Orson. *The Seer*. p. 158. Cited by Jerald Tanner and Sandra Tanner. *Mormonism—Shadow or Reality?* enl. ed. p. 261, Salt Lake City, Utah: Modern Microfilm, 1972.

Religious Truths Defined, p. 175 & 337. Cited by Jerald Tanner and Sandra Tanner. *Mormonism—Shadow or Reality?* p. 64. Salt Lake City, Utah: Modern Microfilm Co., 1964.

Richards, Franklin D., and Little, James A., comp. *A Compendium of The Doctrine of The Gospel*. 2nd ed. Salt Lake City, Utah: Deseret News Company, 1884.

Roberts, B. H. *The Modern Doctrine of Deity*. Salt Lake City, Utah: The Deseret News, 1903.

Roberts, B. H., ed. *History of The Church of Jesus-Christ of Latter-day Saints*. 7 vols. 2nd ed. rev. Salt Lake City, Utah: Deseret News Press, 1963.

Salt Lake Tribune, 24 September, 1972.

Smith, Joseph. *Times and Seasons*. Vol. 5. pp. 613-614. Cited by Jerald Tanner and Sandra Tanner. *Mormonism—Shadow or*

Reality? p. 137. Salt Lake City, Utah: Modern Microfilm, 1964.

Smith, Joseph Fielding. *Doctrines of Salvation.* 3 vols. Compiled by Bruce R. McConkie. Salt Lake City, Utah: Bookcraft, 1956.

Tanner, Jerald and Tanner, Sandra. *Mormonism—Shadow or Reality?* Salt Lake City, Utah: Modern Microfilm, 1964.

Tanner, Jerald and Tanner, Sandra. *Mormonism—Shadow or Reality?* enl. ed. Salt Lake City, Utah: Modern Microfilm, 1972.

Trever, John C. *The Untold Story of Qumran.* Westwood, New Jersey: Fleming H. Revell Company, 1952.

Watt, G. D., ed., *Journal of Discourses.* 26 vols. Liverpool: F. D. & S. W. Richards, 1854; reprint ed., Salt Lake City, Utah, 1966.

Young, Brigham, *Deseret News*, 10 February, 1867. Cited by Ogden Kraut, *Jesus Was Married,* p. 62. Dugway, Utah: by the author, 1970.